Jacky Edwards lives in a gothic mansion in the depths of darkest Somerset, with two peculiar cats who graced her unexpectedly with their presence one fine morning and gracefully consented to stay. Greebs is a foul smelling elderly bag of bones and skin who has a taste for cheese and onion crisps. Grisholm is the feline equivalent of a delinquent teenager with the face of an owl, far too many toes on each foot and a penchant to hide Death's-head moths in the guest bed.

Her husband occasionally passes her on the stairs. She thinks he's grown a beard since she saw him last.

This is her first book.

The Sky is Not The Limit

Jacky Edwards

The Sky is Not The Limit

Vanguard Press

VANGUARD PAPERBACK

© Copyright 2016
Jacky Edwards

The right of Jacky Edwards to be identified as author of
this work has been asserted by her in accordance with the
Copyright, Designs and Patents Act 1988.

ISBN 978 178465 131 2

This is a work of creative nonfiction. The events are portrayed to the
best of the author's memory. While all the stories in this book are true,
some names and identifying details have been changed to protect the
privacy of the people involved.

Vanguard Press is an imprint of
Pegasus Elliot MacKenzie Publishers Ltd.
www.pegasuspublishers.com

First Published in 2016

Vanguard Press
Sheraton House Castle Park
Cambridge England

Printed & Bound in Great Britain

This book is dedicated to my mother. My first inspiration.

Also to my father. My first of many rocks.

To my sisters and brother.
Without them I would have been The Clever One, The Beautiful One, The Delightfully Eccentric One and The Charming One by pure default of being The Only One. But it would have been shockingly lonely and I gladly give up being all those fabulous things for the gift of growing up in their company.

To my Loin Fruit: Katy, Lisa, Sam, Jordyn-Rose, Max and Alfie, my reason for being. (Also my reason for carrying that extra couple of stone and having to nip to the loo quite so often).

Also to Jane. Without whom all this would have been possible, but so very much less enjoyable.

And to my dear husband Paul. In case I never write another one. This one's for you.

Acknowledgements

Firstly. To Jordyn-Rose. The little baby I buried so long ago, who lived for only six weeks but who changed the course of my life forever. I love you sweetheart and I will never forget you.

Secondly my thanks goes to my husband Paul. He saw potential in my scribblings on bits of old envelopes, scruffy receipts and man-size tissues and made me cobble it all together into a tatty manuscript to tout about to publishing houses.

Then to all at Pegasus, particularly Jasmine Molton, who took that tatty manuscript and turned it into this beautiful shiny book with my name on the front that you hold in your hands right now. Wow!

A special round of applause must go to the patients and their families whom it has been my pleasure and honor to care for over the years. You are all so much braver and more resilient than I hope I ever have to be.

Then I shall link metaphorical arms with all the healthcare professionals from every rung of the hierarchical ladder that I have ever had the privilege to work with. We shall close our eyes and sway, and I shall lead us all in a rousing chorus of "We all Stand Together."

To my adult children for their constant reminders that I am supposed to be writing a book and not watching Bake Off, and to my friends, who have stood by my absence with an acceptance bordering on the insulting. Thank you. I'm back. And I have wine.

And lastly to Jane. My co-collaborator, my fellow grand planner and Deputy-in-Chief of My Tribe.

1

It Started With A Dream

We all start our lives dreaming. Firstly of warm milk, full tummies and cuddles and as we grow our dreams change, we look towards the world beyond the home and school room. Our dreams become bigger and sometimes, for some of us, they come true.

I grew up in the seventies when girls still wanted to be nurses and boys wanted to be astronauts. Neither of these paths appealed to me at the time, I was too busy considering the merits of becoming the Wild Woman of Borneo or one of the Moomins and therefore paid scant attentions to the droning on of Mrs Cardboard-Box, my first class teacher, who tried to drum letters and numbers into my head with more patience than I appreciated at the time. Of course, this was way before the now all too common desire of primary school aged children who are waiting to become pop stars and appear on reality shows for a living. But the staring out of the school-room window of disenchanted pupils, busily day dreaming of other things, has probably never changed that much.

My sole engagement in early school life was the free time period where I was only interested in completing my book of favourite things. I whiled away those happy hours pasting pictures of my favourite things, carefully chosen and earnestly gathered from discarded magazines and outdated catalogues into the first book I ever authored, aptly named 'Jacky's Book Of Favourite Things'. I worked methodically, page by page, and dreamed of the day when I could paste the picture of sausages and mash under the heading 'Favourite Food' into the last page of that scruffy tome which contained all the simple things I loved in my tiny, happy life.

Sadly, we moved house just before that long awaited day and I went to a strange new school, friendless and furious that no-one had consulted my five year old self about the change. I'd lost my treasured book of favourite things along the way and it grieved me that it lay somewhere, neglected and incomplete. The grief of that simple loss began an enmity with the educational system that was to last throughout my early years of schooling.

My doting parents saw I wasn't coping and sent me to a small but exclusive private school, where I perfected my art of rebelling against a tough regime. After I'd been expelled for putting my furious foot through all the straw boaters in the cloak room and was sent in disgrace to the local comprehensive, I gave up any serious aspirations of rebellion and simply became lost in that sea of faces, systematically failing to light up any academic skies as those grey years rolled by.

My older sister was The Clever One, with her owlish glasses and quiet double blinks, she observed everything, spoke little and exuded intelligence. My younger sister was always The Beautiful One. Tall and willowy with gorgeous tumbling curls in brown satin with melting chocolate eyes to match. My youngest sister was The Eccentric One, all beads and long dresses teamed with 1920's pork pie hats, she taught herself to speak with cats and was an endless source of fascination to all. My brother was always a golden haired charmer who had the gift of calling all old ladies within a five mile radius to worship at his golden curls and this same gift has seen him well into adult life, never without a string of ladies fluttering at him under long lashes through their half closed eyes. So with all those talents covered, that left me. The Second One.

Teachers who had taught my elder sister before me had eyed me gleefully, 'We'll expect great things from you'. And my heart always sank at these words as it was safe to say they wouldn't get them.

I cringed at the beginning of each school year and I became fairly pitiful at my attempts to fit in.

In a bid to be beautiful, I ironed my frizzy, mouse coloured hair until it stood out at weird right angles from my head, and I experimented with make up, but only succeeded in looking like I'd been drawing on my face.

So I turned my attention to appearing clever. I pretended to write books while actually only filling the pages with circles and colouring them in. I succeeded in being put forward by my hopeful parents for an interview for the prestigious private school which my clever sister already attended on a hard won scholarship. I sat on my hands in front of the scary headmistress with my right angled hair in two right angled bunches, fringe missing, completely burnt off by the iron and

I only managed a stutter and a small belch when asked how my book was coming along.

It was actually coming along marvellously if there was any call for a book full of doodles entitled 'I Hate School'.

I wore a floor length dress, headscarf and beads in an attempt to look artistic and interesting, but I couldn't draw for toffee and just looked like a weird cult leader without the weird cult.

As I got older I even took up smoking in an attempt to be wicked and cool, but I couldn't breathe in that wicked cool smoke and nearly choked to death in front of gorgeous local bad boy Hunky Hunkerson who, quite justifiably, sneered with disdain at my hunched, convulsing body and took my best friend, who had a limp and a pudding bowl haircut, into a disused shed and snogged her instead.

Lucky escape? I hear you, but at the time it just about summed it all up.

So I gave it up pretending to be outstanding and instead when the time came, I wafted away from my school days to the sound of a damp squib, leaving not a ripple of remembrance in my wake, my mind still empty of ambition and my hands bare of any qualifications.

The girls who had wanted to become nurses became nurses and the boys who were to become astronauts became builders and I was nowhere nearer Borneo than Ealing Broadway.

In the absence of any hope or ambition I became a teenage mother to a gaggle of chubby bald babies. I stuffed my large brood, gaggle or herd, or whatever a collection of small children are usually known as (I prefer a stampede myself) under my wing and we set about being poor but happy. And we were.

They were beautiful babies, all fat and wobbly, and who all had hair similar to the tragedy that was my wild barnet. I probably would have been a better mother if I hadn't started pro-creating at the tender age of sixteen. I certainly wouldn't have broken both my wrists by cart-wheeling off a bridge while I was teaching them gymnastics. I wouldn't have ended up with my head in a brace while showing them how to make a springboard out of an old mattress topped with cushions and the splinter filled boards from an orange crate in order to somersault into bed, and I'm sure we would have played less 'hiding from the bailiffs' disguised as a hilarious game of sardines. But then we also wouldn't have celebrated every Sunday with such abandoned joy, even though my babies didn't realise till they were all grown up that Sundays were such a special day because it was the only day the postman didn't come with his heafty sheaf of hopeless brown envelopes. We probably would have had a television and they would have missed out on all our walks to Notting Hill Gate to see the big houses and luscious parks. They may never have discovered the delights of dashing outside to enjoy any passing thunderstorms and see who could catch the most hailstones in their mouths.

All in all, I don't regret not being able to give my babies the financial security they deserved as well as all the accompanying experiences that would have broadened their minds, like foreign travel and flute lessons, but I only really knew for sure that I didn't regret it when my daughter turned to me in the hazy glow of new motherhood after the birth of my first beautiful grand-child and said 'If I can be half the mother to her as you have been to me then we will both be very happy'.

It was then that I evaluated my motherly performance and saw my adult children, all successful and happy, nobody in prison or out tagging bus stops and I knew I'd done as well as I could with the tools I had available and that's all anyone can ask of us. But until that point, how can any of us know. Parenthood doesn't come with a book of instructions. I was merely blessed with youthful ignorance and quite by accident I did a lot of things right.

My dream of nursing did not stir into being until my last little one arrived far too suddenly and too soon. My world shrank to the size of a hard wooden chair and a crib in the bustling Paediatric Intensive Care Unit of a large London hospital, where I sat day after day and watched my tiny baby daughter fade away. Time ground to a halt with the gentle ending of her little life while the cruel world outside kept turning just to insult me.

Alone I laid my child to rest in the hard winter ground and when it was done, I took a long hard breath of the lonely frozen air, closed my eyes and raised my face in desperation to the sky, as one does when one cannot possibly sink further or lose more.

When I opened my bloodshot eyes, sore from weeks of streaming tears an unexpectedly beautiful vista of clear blue sky jolted my vision and a shiver of hope rippled through my battered soul. The thought occurred to me as if for the first time.

"The sky is enormous! Life is enormous! The possibilities are endless and the choices are mine. The sky is the limit, and that's where I'm headed. I'm not sure what I'll do, or how I'll do it or where I'll end up, but one thing is for certain, I'm not staying here!"

2

University

And so at last I had a dream. A proper ambition like all the other kids had had at school. Not a vague desire to live wild among baboons in Borneo, or to transmogrify into a fictional cartoon character, but a proper, rational, reasonable and possibly achievable dream. My new desire for my life was to become a fully qualified, university trained, locally respected and nationally recognised member of the Nursing and Midwifery Council's register of Nursing Practioners. Yes, that's all. A nurse. An ordinary and standard ambition, well within easy reach of others, but for me with my limited education and low self-esteem, not so much.

My resolve set as concrete in my heart as I stomped off home from the lonely funeral of my little girl to my remaining healthy, happy brood, and my fresh ambition stayed in the ground with my lost little one, for a long long time. I only told one person of the plans I had hatched for my future. An old aunt, who laughed scornfully when I eagerly told her that I would become a nurse and move to the country one day.

"Ridiculous" she laughed cruelly "Utterly nonsensical! Look at you. Five children under five, a baby in the ground, living hand to mouth in a council high rise. It's all just grand plans and pipe dreams. You'll do nothing and go nowhere, and that's that".

I was crushed. I tried to rail against her powerful argument. Some angry words attempted to take flight from my gaping mouth but failed before their first flap and sank dismally to dust the threadbare carpet, beneath my too big charity shop shoes as the words failed me. We both knew with absolute certainty that she was right.

I loved being a mother, and I was good at it too, in spite of my youth. The trouble was that I wasn't really very good at anything else. So I put aside my plans and regrets at having such out of reach dreams and put my whole self into motherhood and we all set about the business of growing up together, my babies and me.

I stepped off the world for many years, until my beautiful little fluffy chicks became great big swans with attitude, who flapped their wings in my face, wiped their nose on my head and generally demanded fivers with gay abandon, until the day came when they flew away to begin feathering nests of their own. But always, through those lovely years of chaos and mayhem, at the back of my mind, there was that nagging doubt that I could have achieved a little more.

The trouble was that I was woefully uneducated for any thought of direct entry onto the University course I would need to pass in order to gain my nursing qualification. So once my children had grown I set about doing something about my own self-inflicted ignorance.

I bought some educational children's books from WHSmith and worked my way up the Key Stages.

I dusted off my daughters' old GCSE maths books, looked up the answers to the sums and worked them out backwards until I could understand the formulas to work them out forwards. I threw out my beloved chick lit and allowed myself only the classics as a regular night time read.

In all, I polished my rusty brain for an entire year before nervously introducing it to other recently polished brains at my local college to undertake an Access to Nursing Course, convinced I'd very soon be revealed in my true colours as The Stupid One.

But strangely enough, in that environment, equipped with excellent teachers, skilled in the art of teaching the more mature student, and with an actual focus for my learning, I flowered and passed the course with flying colours. Now here I was, at the grand old age of thirty-four, my first career of motherhood behind me, fresh ink drying on my shiny certificate, on the bus to University with a ticket to my future.

University. A world in between the worlds of work or welfare. An imposing institution where great leaders, professors and politicians could hone their greatness. Where nerds were allowed to be nerdy without threat of a bog water hair wash or the regular wedgies that were often inflicted on the geeks by the coolios at my local comprehensive. Inside these hallowed walls, big glasses and giant rucksacks full of weighty tomes were positively encouraged and anything and everything was possible for those who had the right or the cheek to enter in.

I was definitely of the latter class of entrant, but here I was all the same, on the bus on that great appointed day, clutching my officially headed letter of acceptance onto the University Campus as a student in the Faculty of Nursing and Midwifery. And I was so proud. This day had so long been in my dreams. Granted it wasn't a big dream involving super-stardom, super-modelling or anything with super as its prefix. Although I must, however, confess to the usual hopeful lists compiled in waiting for the day I would finally win The Lottery even though I have never actually played The Lottery in my life. But then I always have been optimistic.

God only knows how I'd actually got in. In fact, I believe they now employ snipers to man the perimeters of the building to keep people like me out. That is, people with atypical formal qualifications who pitch up for interview clutching dusty certificates from Learn Direct and a few dodgy references, but equipped with half a lifetimes' experience and enough enthusiasm to rival any Labrador puppy presented with an entire room of free loo roll and a whole day to kill.

I do understand why entrance to nursing courses have had to be tightened. As professionals we hold the lives and well being of the most vulnerable in our hands and it is so important that only the right hands are chosen for this onerous and awesome task. But I must also trumpet the fact that if my crumpled certificates and boundless enthusiasm had earned my face a look at a very closed door, well then it wouldn't have just been my loss.

As it was, my face shone with anticipation on that short bus journey on my way back into 'school' at the grand old age of thirty four. Surely everyone could see that here was a spring chicken off to University for the very first time, but just in case they missed the maxi-skirt clue, the sensible calf boots, the studious but quite unecesssary lensless glasses perched atop my woolly head, they certainly couldn't miss the University map as I unfolded it to its fullest size and held it up in a pretence of studious scrutiny regardless of the comfort of my neighbouring travel companions who each received an elbow in an ear and a good long look at my big map. I couldn't have drawn more attention if I'd have gone along the rows of passengers and knocked upon each forehead with my new pink pencil case and announced my destination with a song.

I'm sure I heard a chorus of relieved sighs as the bus pulled up outside the University and I disembarked in a flurry of bags, maps, letters, a healthy break-time banana for public consumption and a hidden bag of fun-size Mars bars for a more solitary and satisfactory scoff on the way home.

With no idea where I was actually going, and no more sense of direction than a wayward Tesco's trolley, I actually looked at the map for the first time and confidently set off into that huge confusing compound.

I never heard the feet trotting after me as I strode along the main path so didn't notice that they turned off down the steps just after mine did. I just bowled merrily along, turning left and right, disregarding that giant map in favour of following my gut feelings of where the right lecture hall really should be. I was oblivious to the fact that the second set of footsteps continued after mine until I saw a door I liked the look of and flung it open, intending to insert myself with confidence into the buzzing throng of new nursing students that were all to be my friends.

Striding into a broom cupboard doesn't really have quite the same effect and doesn't usually bring any friends at all, but as I abruptly halted my progress mid-stride, as one does when confronted with the vision of mops and buckets when one was expecting a giant lecture theatre, I was catapulted forward by the owner of the feet that had followed me from the bus.

I whirled around "What the hell are you doing?".

"Errrm, I'm following you. I saw you waving your map about on the bus and you look like you know your way around so I...well...errrm followed you. I hope that's okay. I'm going to be a nurse too".

"Yes it's funny how people always think I know where I'm going, but usually I have no more idea of where I am than an ant in a bee hive. I expect its the way I walk. Well anyway, quick's the word, sharp's the action, if we don't hurry we're going to be late. Chop Chop!" And I strode off again in a different direction, but this time fully aware of the footsteps trotting along behind me.

So although you don't often find friends by hurling yourself into a broom cupboard, this was the very way I met my best friend Jane.

3

Learning Things Other Than Nursing

We all learned a lot that first year and not just about nursing. Jane taught me how to use Powerpoint and create a speadsheet and I taught her how to push into the lunch queue. I gleaned from Gentle Jane the power of catching bees with honey rather than my usual bolshie vinegar and in turn the softly spoken Jane learned quite a few highly imaginative and colourful phrases from me. We became a mighty team of two, complimenting each other in a way that continues to this day.

Now that my years of running around after the children were over, Jane and I took up jogging in order to run off the energy that built up from being so confined during the day, getting up at a ridiculous hour to gasp our way round Puffington Park at daybreak. Together we discovered that stags don't like big red coats and that even though Jane is a good fifteen years younger than me, we both learned that I can shin up a good tree while she is still thrashing about in the long grass. The stag, in turn, found that his rage at the sight of a red coat disappearing up the nearest good tree is no match for the direct glare of the tall, red faced two-legs when it is cornered in the bushes and pulls itself up to a magnificent height and resorts to its steeliest glare. The King of the Forest quickly learned to whistle and tiptoe wisely away.

We also took a lot of road trips that year, to blow off our steam, me in the driver's seat, Jane on navigation. We tried to match our trips to our experiences, such as travelling to Maggots End after witnessing our first post-mortem, visiting Ugley Green when Jane had a skin break out, and finding The Furthest Point of Foulness when I failed my first exam. It does exist. It is far. And it is foul.

For this to happen we had to find a way of supplementing our limited funds. There is a limit to the amount of time a girl can exist on nine pence noodles and not crave a break from that particular taste.

So we delivered telephone directories, papers and pizza in the evenings, became accomplished market researchers at weekends and took on extra duties at the hospital as Health Care Assistants at night, where we could write our essays and assignments during our breaks.

I can't remember sleeping much and we continued with the nine pence noodles, preferring to spend our extra cash on going as far as our petrol and the increasingly weakened suspension of my rickety old car, aptly named The Hagwagon, would take us.

I had always scorned my home country for holidays, not that I'd ever had the chance to go anywhere else, thinking that the England outside London didn't have much to offer except different accents and the same rain. It's true that I had always vaguely wanted to live in the country, but the idea was more consigned to my distant retirement years and linked more to the romantic notion of keeping chickens and going shopping on a bike with a gingham lined wicker basket than any real experience. And it is also true that at this time in my life, I wasn't really finished with the second childhood I was enjoying, not having quite experienced the first.

But on these road trips with Jane, I accidentally discovered how beautiful England is, outside the obvious tourist locations. How different hot buttered toast tastes when the butter is real and the bread still warm and the woman who brings it to you with a smile that's just as real as the butter, and she resembles a large comfortable and cheerful cottage loaf herself.

How friendly folk are outside the Big Smoke. How lovely it is not to have to hide behind a double spread newspaper on The Tube to avoid making eye contact, and a morning greeting with a stranger isn't an invitation to a fight.

And the darkness. I'd never seen true darkness before and my city eyes weren't used to it at all. I was a real danger on the way home after a couple of ciders in a cozy country pub, blundering about in bushes, falling into hedges and ditches and dodging speeding vehicles on the clear and innocent looking, but actually quite lethal, country roads.

But the night sky was a beauty I'd never seen before. I'd stand there in the freezing night, just gazing at the stars and constellations that had been hidden from me till now under a blanket of light pollution. My soul, which itched so ferociously in the classroom, unfurled from its usually crouched and coiled position and learned to relax and chew a strand of metaphorical grass under those majestic country night skies, where billions of light years lazily whispered an ancient wisdom that in a hundred years we will all be dust and they will still be there and nothing that happens is really worth worrying about at all.

To someone of a more pessimistic nature, this realisation may have been their cue to waft away into a low cloud and simply not bother as any effort at all would surely come to mean nothing in the end. But to me, with my sunny and optimistic disposition, it simply meant the freedom to leap.

I may indeed curl up into a foetal cringe ball replaying my failures and shame with boring regularity, but they surely live longer in my mind than anybody else's. If we were all destined for the ash heap then at least I was going to land there in a cloud-burst of purple dusty glory, having barged through every door, grasped every opportunity with both eager paws and made the absolute most of everything life had to offer while it was still being offered.

4

Making the Most of it.

During the last two years of student life we settled down to more serious studying. I was becoming exposed to more and more learning opportunities. Well, if you pardon the phrase, I set about exposing myself to new learning opportunities.

Working as a student nurse on any ward or department for twelve weeks every term was a gift of variable quality.

I was not employed by the hospital, but rather sent by the University, assigned to a particular ward for three months. I was not counted into staff numbers on any shift and certainly during the first two placements of the first year I was happy to noodle along after the Healthcare Assistants, learning the basics, because I truly knew absolutely nothing.

By the second year, I could find my way around a good sluice or a patient kitchen. I had a good idea of the day-to-day running of any ward and thanks to my extra work as a Healthcare Assistant working for the Staff Bank of nurses and assistants in my spare hours, I had quite a lot more experience than most in my rank. So I decided to really push my placements in the last two years. I needed to learn some more advanced nursing skills ready for the still distant time when the keys were placed into my hands and I would be left to sink or swim on my own as the staff grade nurse I had always wanted to be.

The trouble was, that the wards I was assigned to as a student nurse, always seemed to be short of substantive staff. No matter which shift I was rostered for, I always appeared to be desperately needed for actual work, as a cross between a glorified domestic, ward hostess, assistant clerk, low grade healthcare assistant, runner, gopher, invisible helping hand and scapegoat operating outside the safety net and comfort enjoyed by the folk who joyfully delegated the most menial or unpleasant tasks to me and my ilk.

I would go around giving bed baths to patients who couldn't wash themselves, bowls of warm water to those who could. I would help patients to walk to the bathrooms for their morning toilette and give bedpans and bottles to those who couldn't. I would dish out the breakfasts, toast with jam or marmalade, cereals and hot drinks and then clear it all away while looking longingly at the staff nurse on the morning drug round efficiently swinging her big wooden trolley around the ward, reading prescriptions, and doling out the right medications at the right dose, to the right patients at the right time, while wearing a super cool fluorescent tabard proclaiming DO NOT DISTURB! NURSE DOING DRUGS! or some similar instruction. I was desperate to be included, to start reading real prescriptions and matching the correct medications from the seemingly bottomless wooden trolley on its four wobbly wheels. I always asked if I could help with this important task, not being one to hold back when I could just as easily come forward, but the answer would always be a vague wave of the hand and a promise of maybe tomorrow.

As a student nurse I might, and certainly did, think that I was all that and a bag of chips, but to the nurses on the ward I was part way between a volunteer and a bloody nuisance.

So I decided to take matters into my own tentacles. We were allowed and even positively encouraged by our student faculty, if not by the staff we would cheerfully leave to struggle without us, to take advantage of any studious hospital activity for which we had particular interest in and, more importantly, if those in charge of it would have us. So I sat down with the big green hospital internal telephone directory and ran my finger down its laminated pages to find something else to do to fill my time and my brain.

I went out for a day with the Stoma Nurse, and wore a stoma bag filled with warm hot chocolate on my stomach next to my skin. I was so self-conscious of it leaking (which it did) or bursting (which it also did) that ever since that day I have always loved a good, well attached stoma and feel an immense respect for those who have to wear the bag for real.

I spent a day in the diabetic clinic, but all those charts and books detailing the minutiae of what someone had eaten on a particular day next to a column of how much insulin they had needed to control their blood sugar as a result of it, went on and on, day after day. I was so bored, and even though I take my figurative hat off to the nurses who define this as their field, and to their patients who are so good at writing in those books and filling in these charts and in the main take as much care of themselves as an athlete would have to in order to stay healthy. Yes my hat is firmly off and I have dropped into a deep respectful curtsey to honour them all; but that branch of nursing is just not for me.

The microbiology lab was quite the reverse. I had arranged my day there because no one would have me anywhere else, but I ended up having a rather fascinating time. I had the obligatory sample lecture, about what happens to incorrectly or inadequately labelled samples (they go straight in the bin) and I dipped my metaphorical toe into the muddy waters of medical law to find out why that is, before immediately moving on to the juicy stuff. How does a snail get into a bladder? Why does a snail want to get into a bladder? Tapeworms. How long do they really grow and is it worth buying one off the internet and swallowing it on purpose to help one shift that stubborn last half stone? I mean, you can't get away from the fact that the microbiology lab is just a huge white room filled with test tubes containing the most revolting things the human body has to offer, with just a smidgeon of the animal community thrown in, but once you get these people going they have some brilliant stories to tell. While I was there one of the scientists had just had a full-to-the-brim sample jar of the most offensive diarrhoea explode into his face, which was at the time sporting the fullest ginger beard you could get through a door with. The note that circulated the wards immediately after this event, warning all against the perils of over filling sample bottles, belied the hilarity behind the event. The story was repeated endlessly and enjoyed by all, except maybe the poor lab technician who forever after went clean shaven to work.

Yes we all think anybody that works full-time as a scientist in a laboratory must be a super boffin of the first water, probably a little autistic, live in a freezing garrett, or everlastingly with their mum and only be able to get along with their own kind, but these dedicated folk have a vibrant sense of humour all their own and I thoroughly recommend spending a day with them if you ever get the chance.

It was through this back door that I got to see my first post mortem. I was very eager, being possessed of a slightly morbid trait by nature, combined with a fascination for the human body in all its perfection and destruction.

I rang the mortuary on the off chance that my eagerness and student status would buy me a ticket to witness this usually most private of hospital activity, but the mortuary technicians were surprisingly welcoming, and as long as the pathologist in charge of the next suitable case granted permission, I was in.

The call came one afternoon while I was busy with the small team of dedicated Health Care Assistants metaphorically painting the Seventh Bridge, which is how we referred to the checking and changing of all the bed-bound patients on this large medical ward. It mainly served to house long-term elderly patients who were medically fit for discharge but, due to their deteriorating mental and physical abilities, were unable to return home and were awaiting beds in longer term care facilities, rehabilitation wards or nursing homes.

I usually enjoyed this part of the job, however distasteful it may seem to the uninitiated. Yes there was a lot of clearing up of the usual human waste product, both in solid and liquid form, but I have a real soft spot for the elderly and found this a time to connect with them individually and in a more leisurely fashion than the usual fly past with a tea trolley.

I really did find it an honour to be trusted with the basic needs of these old folk and took time and trouble to make sure that they were left clean, comfortable and as happy as possible before moving on to the occupant of the next bed.

This all took a phenomenal amount of time and as soon as we had finished it was time to start again, which, although I enjoyed the ask in the main, could be a tad soul destroying, so when the call came from the mortuary to say that I had been granted permission to attend a post mortem the following morning, I was delighted to take a break from that usual ward routine.

I arrived the following morning, in a freshly ironed and starched student nurse uniform and rang the bell fixed to the outside of an anonymous looking grey building hidden at the back of the hospital so it was hidden from public view in strangely plain sight.

I had cycled past it many times but it had never quite registered on my radar as being a place of any importance. If pressed, I may have considered it to be a storage facility where patients' old notes were kept, or an ancient burial ground for defunct medical equipment, rusty beds or mouldering mattresses awaiting disposal, and of no interest to me whatsoever.

But suddenly this building took on an air of great importance, and it is sure that I never passed it by again without a respectful silence for the practitioners who work there and the ex-human remains who pass through its doors.

After showing my identification and donning a white coat, I joined the two female mortuary technicians in the large white clinical room where the mottled naked body of a man lay, in stark contrast to the clinical white glare of the room.

I was briefly shocked by the lack of dignity shown to this dead man, merely because life had been pronounced extinct and I had to swallow a few times to try and clear the bitter odour that cloyed in my throat as a distinctive taste, which I have never been able to forget. This was death, not as I had seen it, in the transition phase from life, but cold, congealed death that almost solidified in the air.

With a deep steadying breath I stepped up and stood next to the corpse, out of the way of the technicians as they got to work, opening first the abdomen and chest, from pelvis to throat, cracking the ribs to expose the heart and lungs, and finally removing the top part of the skull to form a window through which to remove the brain.

This was not a business for the faint hearted, but as I watched, my revulsion and nausea gave way to an overwhelming feeling of wonder and miracle.

As I held the human brain in my two gloved hands I held a personality, a perfect individual essence. A lifetime of memories, experiences, loves and losses, expertise and skills gained before I was born. Here in my hands was the driving force of the man whose vehicle lay flayed open on the table. I was in awe.

The pathologist entered and the lesson I was there to learn began. He sliced up the various organs that had been lined up on the table for his inspection, in order to determine the cause of death. He was extraordinarily patient as he dissected the body parts slowly for my benefit and pointed out the fatal flaws in human biology that affected the lungs, heart and brain to such an extent as to extinguish life.

I think I started to believe in God that day, or at least a force greater than an accidental bang. All of the necessities that control the functions of us all, so neatly packed and protected, so intricately wired and balanced, and so robust as to last for eighty years and more. It was nothing less than majestic. To replicate just the intestinal tract, which turns a plateful of delicious bacon sandwich into a simple tube of human waste with all the technology available to the mighty brains in existence today, still requires a room the size of a small aircraft hangar filled with steaming things, whistling things and chugging things reminiscent of Willy Wonka's Chocolate Factory, to reproduce. And yet here, in just one small dedicated area of the human body, this wonderful system does just that, nestled under the pump that drives it all; which is under the living computer which programmes and maintains it all, above the things that clean it all; surrounded by a puzzle of bone which supports, protects and moves it all; held together by a layer which contains it all; connected by amazing highways and networks that allow these separate entities to exist in complete harmony with each other. And the most amazing thing of all is that all of this happens without us actually thinking about it at all. Wow! What is not to love.

I learned more about human anatomy and physiology and the process of disease in that one day than in any lecture or course undertaken before or since and as the morning drew to its close, the gentleman's organs were placed back into their rightful place, his post mortal wounds sutured, he was dressed for burial and he was suddenly human again. I found myself silently offering up a prayer of thanks to the soul of this man, who had taught me so much and I returned to the ward, grateful for the experience, but also very glad to be back amongst the living.

5

A Brand New Nurse.

And just like that, it was over.

The safe University doors we had come to love, as well as hate, had swung shut on us forever.

Our student uniform tunics had been joyfully burned along with our subscriptions to the Student Nursing Times and our giant tutorial books, with their spines largely uncracked. These were resigned to a far more useful retirement of propping up wobbly coffee tables and bed corners, or otherwise were sold to fund celebrations of cheap yet exuberant proportions.

Job applications were sent and the replies nervously awaited. Smart yet sensible shoes were bought and charity shops were scoured for clothes suitable for interviews for our first ever, real life, paid nursing jobs.

Our minds were cleared of all else while we sought to cram up on information governance, NICE guidelines, Health and Safety in the Workplace Acts and key issues from the most recent governmental White Paper.

Coffee shops were crammed with ex-nursing students, muttering rehearsed answers to the inevitable questions that seem to have no sensible scripted response. Being asked what my strengths are remains easy enough, never being one to have to search for my light under any bushels, but the point of being asked about my weaknesses is a standard interview question that still baffles me as to its complete uselessness. Does my partiality for a triple Archers and lemonade on my evenings off count as a weakness, and will my propensity to lateness win me any fans? I think not.

This question seems to be intended to weed out the tellers of truth from those of us with the ability to weave a tale of a character flaw which can be seen as a triumph within the strange world of the nursing profession. After many internal struggles with this particular question, and no help from my equally baffled colleagues on the matter, I eventually settled to confess the trait that I become bored fairly easily and therefore would like to commit myself to constant study and skill updates in order to overcome this devastating flaw and remain the most dedicated nurse in the fleet.

I have stuck with this stock answer for many interviews in the intervening years between then and now, and if it has been uttered with my tongue firmly in my cheek, then it has certainly been received with the same from many interviewers. So I can be left with the firm belief that this is the most stupid and unhelpful interview question in the history of stupid and unhelpful interview questions, and should I ever be in the position to bestow or deny gainful employment to another quaking practitioner, I shall do us all a favour and leave that particular line of questioning unexplored. But I digress.

A leaping up from coffee shop seats, punches in the air and shouts of 'YES!' soon replaced the pacings and mutterings, as one by one, we left the safety of the coffee shops that had been our regular haunt throughout our student years. No doubt the common practice of sharing of one extra large cappuccino, coupled with the request for five spoons and the ability to make that one coffee last a whole afternoon, made our exits a relief to those understanding baristas as we left their comforting prescence for the brave new world of gainful employment.

The full weight of responsibility took a while to settle onto my shoulders as I went straight into the reasonably safe and relatively protected world of intensive care nursing, while my friends and colleagues went largely onto the rock face of the wards where they were invariably handed a huge bunch of keys and eight patients of varying degrees of sickness and left to get on with it.

Any first year nurse could usually be found by following the sound of sobbing to the nearest linen cupboard or storeroom.

I'll never forget swinging through the hospital corridors late one night, on a fruitless errand to find tartan paint or a skyhook or some such jolly japery I was yet to realise I had fallen victim to, in my brand new scrubs and clogs, with a lunatic smile on my face and the confident stride of someone who was convinced they were Jack the Biscuit, when in the dim distance of the hall a very different creature lurched into view.

Tall yet stooped, exhaustion hung around its frame and the lights seemed to extinguish in line with the slow progress of this zombie. My eyes strained to get a better view. I had never seen anything like this creature walking upright.

As we came alongside, the sheet of lank hair that partially covered that grey face parted as that poor beast of burden lifted its woeful gaze to meet my curious eyes.

It was Jane.

I hadn't seen her since she had secured a job on the Clinical Assessment Unit, and though this area of nursing is a fantastic breeding ground for all the acute specialities to feed from in their constant demand for new nursing staff with their reputation for speed, efficiency and grace under fire, this is undoubtedly the hardest area of all in which to learn these skills.

Poor Jane.

I had it easy by comparison.

I was birthed gently into my nursing life. It was weeks before I was left alone in charge of a single patient, and a whole year of intense theory and practice before I was considered worthy of any opinion.

That's not to say there were no challenges for me. Learning to support the human body's distinctly separate systems using external equipment is difficult and it takes time to achieve the required high standard of competence and confidence but, by mid-winter I was getting there, a fledgling nurslet in Intensive Medicine. Clumsy and uncoordinated but definitely ready to leave the nest and fly solo.

I can never forget my first Christmas Night in Intensive Care.

Mrs White, the Vicar's wife, was admitted from one of the wards after being struck down by a flu-like illness some days before. She was a previously healthy young woman, in her early forties, and her demise was swift and cruel.

The virus she had caught went straight to her heart, filling that organ with fluid, which rendered it unable to pump effectively. By the time she came to us she was beginning to lose the pressure of her blood which affected the oxygen supply to her brain so she was, in turns, agitated and drowsy.

We initiated a medical coma with powerful anaesthetic drugs administered through a long line that entered the jugular vein in her neck and quickly commenced full life support with artificial ventilation from a respirator. Her blood pressure was supported with powerful vessel constrictors, which squeezed the precious blood from her limbs and concentrated it into her vital organs in the hope that this would give her immune system time to rally and fight the organism which was attacking its host.

As soon as she was stabilised, a still pale figure in an artificial sleep that belied the battle going on within that ominously calm exterior, her husband was called from the waiting room to take his seat by her side.

He was deathly pale himself, with dark circles under his eyes matching the black square of his collar of office, his hair sticking up at the back, his shirt and trousers crumpled from his long night in a plastic orange chair, opposite a clock he couldn't take his eyes from, as it ticked his married life away.

He dropped into the chair that had been brought to the bedside for his vigil, he grasped the almost lifeless hand of his wife with both of his so their wedding rings touched and his weary head rested on their three fiercely interlocked hands and he quietly started to pray.

All that Christmas Night he kept faith with his soul mate and his muttered prayers to his Celestial Master provided a constant and desperate monotone as the tears ran endlessly down his face onto the still white hand of his fading other half.

There was to be no Christmas Miracle for them.

The Vicar's Wife passed from this world with the darkness leaving a desolate husband and two bewildered children behind her and there was nothing any of us could do despite all our combined medical knowledge and the all the brilliance and expertise of the team gathered in the span of time since the beginning of conscious human existence.

It was at that awful moment that I realised for the first time that we are not magic people. We cannot give life and we cannot take it away, we can only perform some limited human business in between.

The Santa hats we had bounced into work with just the evening before lay in a sad little pile in the staff room and we had all removed the novelty jingle bell earrings which were the custom at Christmas in that place. The Christmas sweets and chocolates, bought for us by patients and relatives lucky enough to have something to be grateful for, stayed untouched on the central nurses' station as somehow none of us had the taste for celebrating Christmas any more.

The New Year brought new patients, new miracles and new tragedies but I have never forgotten my first Christmas as a fully fledged Intensive Care nurse, which will always belong to The Vicar's Wife.

That New Year, however, was to bring with it one of the finest triumphs I have ever been directly involved in.

Mrs Iron Grey was a prison officer, also in her early forties when she arrived in Intensive Care during the first wave of the Swine Flu epidemic.

She wasn't the first case of H1N1 that we had seen, and she certainly wasn't the last, but she was easily the most memorable; at least to me.

She was as sick as anybody I have ever seen still living. Her newly fragile lungs blew new holes every day which we punctured further with drainage tubes in a bid to re-inflate them, while her other organs sacrificed themselves to failure in order to salvage her brain as the sepsis overwhelmed her mortal frame. Her system became so fragile we were unable to even move her position in bed to prevent the inevitable pressure sores which come from lying inert and skeletal on bony prominences for any period of time

She was kept in the artificial sleep of the soul, in twilight between life and death, as we used every power in our arsenal to support each organ as they failed in turn.

Day after day, night after night the battle for her life continued, and for every inch of ground we gained, we lost another.

Her life partner of twenty years could do nothing but fiddle with the hem of her long black cardigan as she watched and waited for each agonising day to pass from her position in the now familiar orange plastic chair at her Lady's bedside.

Slowly, ethical considerations began to creep in and discussions were begun as to whether it might be futile and therefore cruel to continue with such aggressive procedures and therapies as Miss Grey was enduring on a daily basis and the question of the quality of life she could expect if she did survive began to be raised.

The general consensus among the eminent medical experts in charge of her case, in discussion with equally eminent medical experts from Centres of Excellence in Respiratory Intensive Care Medicine around the country was that her overall chances of survival were growing increasingly slim with every passing day and if she miraculously survived long enough to be discharged from hospital she would likely spend the rest of her life as a respiratory cripple, chained to a domiciliary ventilator and tied to the mercies of community carers until a final chest infection took mercy upon her soul and carried her ravaged body from this world to the next.

The decision to withdraw treatment is a heavy one for any Intensive Care Consultant Team, weighted with 'what ifs' and I for one don't envy the brave makers of that decision at all. On one hand, to opt to continue to brutally extend anothers torment far beyond that which we would allow an animal to suffer in the hope of a miracle, which none can deny might happen one time in one million, while others might argue that to withdraw the heroics, crank up the analgesia and prepare the family of that precious human life for a definite death in denial of that million-to-one chance is an unenviable position to aspire to, and I have the utmost respect for those who choose to take on that grim mantle.

What a dilemma!

Mrs Iron Grey's previous good health, excellent fitness level and undoubtedly robust reserves, which had carried her thus far, increased her odds of survival marginally enough for these arguments to bounce back and forth for several more weeks, as Mrs Iron Grey clung to life by a thread.

The situation looked hopeless to us all and Miss Grey's partner took on the appearance of a spectre herself as the seemingly endless watching and waiting took its toll while her loved one's life ebbed away.

Then one of the young Consultants came across a paper detailing a new treatment that was delivering astonishing results in some of the most desperate cases of this kind.

This involved using a lung bypass machine which could oxygenate the patients' blood and feed their vital systems while allowing the lungs to deflate and rest completely until such time as they could recover from their insult and healing could take place.

Our medical team lost no time in referring Miss Grey and she was quickly accepted and transferred to the nearest specialist facility. By this time she had been with us for nearly five months and we missed her and her partner keenly, although regular updates from the specialist centre kept us informed of her condition which seemed to remain stable enough to keep her future perilously uncertain.

During this time, although other cases took her place, and came and went and went and came, I became restless. My knowledge base had increased considerably and I began to look around for bigger and more exciting pastures to graze in.

I soon found a position in a heavingly large and fast paced Intensive Care Unit in Central London, which specialised in trauma and it was with mixed feelings that I gave in my notice at the small District General Hospital that had seen me through my student days and given me my first chance.

I looked forward to my future with increasing excitement while saying my goodbyes to my colleagues who had started as my mentors and had become my friends. My timing was unusually brilliant as it was in my very last week that news of Miss Grey came at last. That amazing lady had recovered completely, been discharged home to convalesce and would be returning to light duties at the prison on the same day as I started my new job. I don't think I was alone in feeling hot tears prick my eyes when I heard this. I truly felt part of a team that had performed a miracle against all the odds and I bounced out of the hospital on that day with a huge smile on my face, looking forward to placing my foot eagerly on the next rung of the ladder.

There was, however to be one more memorable night.

6

I Remember the Night
Michael Jackson Died

It was an unremarkable mid-summer night at the hospital. Still dark and cold outside, but in the warmth of the Intensive Care Unit, we nurses busied ourselves with the tasks of the night shift which, in that particular speciality, is much the same as the day shift but without the routine procedures, consultant ward rounds, updates with relatives and visiting hours. With plenty of emergency admissions and the usual unexpected events to take their place we were not expecting to be bored.

As we buzzed steadily on, we gradually became aware of an external fissure of electricity on the customary grapevine of quiet chatter and harmless gossip that goes on among nursing staff during those subdued night time working hours. And then suddenly, with the entrance of an external nosy parker from another department, the news broke and the shock was upon us.

"Guess what! Michael Jackson's dead!"

"No!"

"Yes!"

"How do you know?"

"Sister Blister just told me in the corridor while I was getting a coke from the vending machine!"

"Don't be daft, he can't be, he's only young. He's about to go on tour and I've got tickets for the first night!"

"I don't think he cares about that, well, not if he's dead anyway."

"Right. Get the radio!"

The radio was duly brought and tuned in to the nearest news station as we gathered around it hoping for some conclusive news. This was a highly unusual practice as we liked to keep the unit as dark and quiet as possible to preserve our patient's sense of night and day intact, but here was a sniff of some VERY BIG NEWS and we just had to know.

Within minutes it was official.

It was true. Michael Jackson, the musical hero of all our childhoods, whose music most of us had grown up with, practised our first choreographed dance steps to, tasted our first sip of illicit alcohol and kissed our first boy to. Some of us had wanted to marry him and some of us had wanted to be him, but all of us had had posters of him up on our teenage bedroom walls and had worshipped this colossal, larger than life character. He had divided us when accused of some truly heinous crimes and divided us further with his later acquittal. We had peered at the close-ups of his collapsing face and we had all offered theories and insights into his strange lifestyle and eccentric ways. We had all been united with the eventual news that our hero was back on form and back on tour and we all set our alarms and boosted our signals on the morning the tickets had gone on sale, joy for those whose lightening fingers and fortunate timing had secured them a ticket, disappointment and unashamed jealously for those not so lucky.

And now he was dead. We stared at each other eyes wide, *blink blink* and then without a further thought I turned and ran from the room to find Jane.

I swiped my way out of the unit, flew down the darkened corridors, and hurled myself down the stairwell three stairs at a time, leaping over the last five of each flight as I raced down to the second floor from the sixth.

Down another dark corridor, the automatic lights being unable to keep up with me, I didn't stop until I reached the Clinical Assessment Unit where Jane was working.

I skidded into the ward and stopped breathlessly at the staff room where I leaned against the open door panting with exertion.

"Where's Jane?"

A bored face looked disinterestedly up at me from an enormous pile of patients' notes and a vague wave of the hand gestured towards the side ward that branched off from the main.

"Down the side." The yawn at the end was, if not actually performed, most definitely implied

My feet carried me fast around the corner in search of my friend and I shout whispered as quietly and urgently as I could, as I ran towards a light and the sound of activity coming from a bay at the far end.

"Jane! Jane! Guess what!"

I flung open the doors with all the restraint available to me, which wasn't a lot, with the announcement "Bloody hell Jane, Michael Jackson's dead!"

Five elderly faces looked up at me from five of the beds that occupied the six bedded bay while the whole cardiac arrest team stopped what they were doing and looked up at me from the sixth with a perfectly synchronised "No!"

Time stood absolutely still for what seemed like minutes, but in reality was more like a nano-second, as my sudden entrance and shocking news froze the frenetic activists in their determined battle with The Reaper. It was a grimly comical scene.

The patient lay flat, deathly white skin tinged with blue, contrasting with the large black pads stuck to his chest in readiness to charge his heart with a bolt of electricity and shock it back to life. Large bore needles bristled in his veins ready to receive the burst of adrenaline that would strengthen his shocked heart back into a regular rhythmic beat.

Time seemed to still as the medical and nursing team froze in their individual activities, Jane in blue scrubs was wandering about with a pile of medical notes while an old nurse with white hair stood at the head end holding a mask full of oxygen over the face of the nearly departed, while an older medic knelt on the bed, hands crossed and poised over the patients' chest, the compressions interrupted, which would hopefully manually pump his heart with enough force to send enough oxygenated blood to his brain. A young doctor stood at the defibrillator, his hand on the dial that would measure the charge and a few other people whose faces blurred into each other as they stood with bags of fluid, vials of drugs and charts to record all the furious activity that would be taking place had I not barged in.

Eyes wide. Mouths open. Blink blink.

The collective chorus of shocked voices met my announcement with the by now expected "No!" and the silence stretched as I took in the scene.

"Oh God... Okay... no... errrr... carry on."

My words cut the silence and broke the spell and all the usual frenetic activity that accompanies a cardiac emergency suddenly re-erupted as everyone remembered at once what they were doing and why they were there. Nobody noticed as I slunk out of the room and made my way back to the unit to carry on my night's work, the shock of the night's events still fresh and a wedge of sadness in my heart for that talented young man who never knew me but whom I grew up with nevertheless.

As for the patient whose resusitation attempt was interrupted, albeit only briefly, by this world breaking news, he was admitted to the Intensive Care Unit later that night and successfully roused from a medically induced coma a few days later after we managed to gain control of the condition which had originally caused his heart to stop.

When he recovered enough to sit up in bed with a nice cup of tea while awaiting a bed back on the medical ward, the buzz that had reached us all the week before finally found him.

"Didn't you hear? Michael Jackson's dead?"

His eyes wide. Two blinks.

"No!"

7

Suicide

The pulse of this place was palpable as I nervously crept in to the crowded staff room and took my place at the back on my first day in this large impressive place, that enjoyed the reputation of being one of the best Trauma Centre's in the whole of London.

The frisson of excitement that fizzed under my initial trembling nausea of the new girl never left me in the whole of the time I worked there. It was a place where miracles were possible and professional growth was inevitable, as was the personal diminishment of my life outside those great old walls as the job gradually took over my life.

Although I've long forgotten who said the words spoken to me by some wise old soul on that first day, the words themselves are burned into my forebrain forever.

"You'll have fun, and you'll learn loads, but the burnout rate for nurses here is high and the average time they last is about two years, so enjoy it while it lasts. The clock is ticking". And so it was.

The demographics here were different than the less diverse mix I was used to in my patient group at my previous hospital, which was centered in the leafy suburbs. Though it served its fair share of the less fortunate population, a large number of our patients had been of working class and an even greater slice of our patient pie chart was made up of elderly folk.

Here in the heart of London Central was home to the most impoverished of people, often living outside the law and below the poverty line. This was a transitory populace of mainly young people from all corners of the globe and representing all colours and cultures, mostly on their way to somewhere else, sometimes by design and often by the necessity to remain as invisible as possible to the beady eye of the powers that be.

Guns, knives, drugs, crime and anger ruled those dangerous dark streets and provided the grease for a slippery slope for many young folk, who found my colleagues and I at the bottom waiting to catch them in the safety net of that grand old building, which had served to catch the unfortunate members of the areas social underclass for centuries.

So they were caught. If they were lucky.

Their stories are plentiful and tragic for the pointlessness and savagery of their circumstances and tainted with an extra sadness because of their usually tender youth.

Lonely Girl was in her early twenties when she came into my care, having spent her younger years living in the bosom of her large Jamaican family in a three roomed tenement, on the seventh floor of a grim high rise hidden deep in the squalor of this concrete jungle, decorated loudly with anti-everything graffiti, shrouded in a constant mist of the stench of old urine and the rather more subtle undertone of despair.

Despite these surroundings the family thrived, avoiding many of the pitfalls that gaped around them due to the presence of an archetypal mother, who nurtured her brood on a diet of an ever full dutchie pot on the stove, a close extended church family and endless love that surrounded them all and kept them safe.

Lonely Girl had been the quiet child of the family, happy to blend into the background and observe the raucous play of her rowdy sisters. Possibly because of this inherent trait nobody noticed as her placid nature gave way to a deep anxiety and crippling self-doubt and as she grew into puberty, mental illness quietly stole her mind.

She began to hear voices in her early teens and gradually withdrew further and further into her room and into her shell as her noisy family bustled around her and her inner voices grew louder in their cruel torments.

One normal winter's evening, as the family gathered round the large dining table for food and communion, amidst the usual chatter and laughter Lonely Girl stood up, walked calmly over to the window, and leapt out.

If she had landed on her head, I would never have known her, but as it so often happened, she landed on her feet which folded up into her body splintering her bones and shattering her spine.

The air medics operated on poor Lonely Girl's destroyed body on the roadside where she fell. They split her broken chest and an expert hand manually pumped her heart as they fought to save her. The team managed to stabilise her to the point where she may just survive the scoop and run to the waiting helicopter and as that window of opportunity opened just a crack, they strapped her body to the stretcher, grabbed a corner each, and leapt into the helicopter, which lifted them into that black starless night and brought her to me.

Lonely Girl did survive that hellish journey through the air. She survived her admission to Intensive Care and survived the many many operations over many many weeks to fix the body that was forever separated from the instructions of the brain that was supposed to control it.

She eventually opened her eyes and slowly took in her new sterile surroundings, with that aseptic smell peculiar to the hospital environment and all the constant bleeps, blips, clangs and bangs that naturally accompany that unnatural scent.

She gazed in turn at each face of her shell shocked family who had stood with her during the dark nights of her soul's struggle and they held her paralysed body through the gradual dawning of the realisation that she would never again have the choice to end her own torment. The rest of her life would be spent waiting for the end. A single tear made its way over her scarred cheek and ran down her neck to nestle in the indent of her collarbone, where she lost all sensation of its warm, wet and comforting existence.

I have the deepest sympathy for those whose life has become so intolerable that they choose to end it and the overwhelming sadness I feel for those tortured souls has never lessened with my frequent exposure to their stories. One of the three wishes I would request from the genies of my childhood games would be for a time machine so I could go back and intervene in every suicide mission I have ever had the misfortune to be involved in, arriving just before they hurl themselves into that final oblivion.

"No wait!"

"It will get better, I promise it will."

Even to my ears, which are well used to accepting my grand plans, this one sounds empty, hollow and probably deeply ineffective in the face of the desolation that must be felt by those whose only desire left in this life is to end it.

Maybe I can only really be useful after the event, if it has not been carried out quite to completion.

This role is unsatisfying, as to save the body when you cannot save the mind it houses, is usually just the recipe for disaster, and, just in this particular arena a great sadness for the patient's future usually accompanies the cure.

De Icer Man entered my consciousness on a hospital trolley, on a grey, untroubled day, where nothing much was happening in Intensive Care except the usual hum of the continued business of the day, and the odd gossipy conversation to break the unusual monotony.

He was semi-conscious, shivering under a sheet, having purposefully drunk de-icer in a bid to do as much damage to himself as possible.

Not a great deal of de-icer needs to be consumed in order to turn the blood to acid, whereupon life will quickly become extinct. De Icer Man had nearly drunk enough, but not quite.

We had to work quickly.

The only way to save his life was to put him to sleep, pump the anti-dote into him continuously, while filtering his blood through an extra corporeal circuit and hope for the best.

It took a long time to bring that boy back from the brink, but it was only when he was safe on the shore of this world that the true tragedy of his tale began to unfold.

His only possession on admission was a voluminous and extremely gaudy ladies handbag.

That was the first clue. This and the silky French undies that nestled next to his skin under the dirty jeans and filthy t-shirt, which had been cut from him as we began the task of saving his life, pointed to a deep and hidden battle with his sexuality and a deeply confused sense of self.

The stripes of varying shades of healing that covered his arms and legs from slashes with a blade held in his own hand spoke of an all consuming self-hatred while the older silvery slashes that decorated his back and buttocks told a far more sinister tale of childhood abuse, while x-rays revealed an unexpected and shocking finding even to us, hard practitioners on the rock face of a wicked world.

This poor boy had inserted pins, needles and other sharp metal objects deep into his hated testicles and this more than any other discovery bore witness to a pain so deep that it would melt the heart of an iceberg.

His handbag revealed a diary of self-harm going back years and spoke of this tortured soul's intolerable existence, whose torment found a transitory relief only through the letting of his own blood.

All the components of a life lived below the nets that were supposed to catch him were hinted at in this pitiful diary of a young man's complete misery.

Poverty, depravity, hard drugs and hard men had shaped this child into the man that lay before us, and as the battle for his life commenced, there was not a single one of us who did not know in our heavy hearts that although we may yet win this battle, we had already lost the war.

Suicide, for us at the sharp end, was blunted by the gift of distance from the weight of the suffering that causes us to meet it head on.

Mr Farley Barleymow was such a case in point. His was an all too familiar story that we could all sympathise with on a personal level.

He was a simple country farmer, working the land which his father and his father's father had worked before him, with the land yielding less and less bounty as each generation tried to make their living from the earth in an ever-changing world.

The Barleymow family had a son who worked along side his father and the wisdom of all his ancestors was passed on to this only son as he prepared to take his father's place one day.

He taught him about how to scrape a living from the land, which crops to grow year on year, how to cultivate them, how to sell them, who to sell them to and how to prepare the ground for the next harvest.

All Mr Barleymow's pride lay in that land and his desire to pass it on to his son as a working concern, as his father had passed it on to him.

Afterwards none of the family could pinpoint the exact situation that drove Mr Barleymow over the edge. Maybe it wasn't any one thing, maybe it was a constant drip. Enough of those will drown a man in the end.

Anyway, Farmer Barleymow started to drown and his family took a while to notice.

He began to work late into the night, and his wife woke often to find his side of the bed empty, but she put it down to the erratic lifestyle of farming life and went back to sleep.

His family became concerned when his weight loss became obvious, his gaunt face and his haunted eyes sinking into the dry skin of his face, but unbekwownst to them, it was already too late.

One morning, Master Giles the Farmer's Son, was awoken by the baying of the cows. Wondering why his father hadn't milked them before he left for the fields as he always did, he stumbled out of bed and made his way through the dewy freshness of the early morning and swung open the door of the barn to find his father's body swinging by the neck from the barn's sturdy centre beam.

I cannot imagine the agony felt by that poor boy. It is said that the things which will knock us floorwards will not be the things we expect and prepare for, but rather we will be blindsided on a random Tuesday morning, and this is what happened to Mr Giles The Farmer's Son when he found his father just in time to be too late.

There was a barely detectable thready pulse in Mr Barleymow's twitching body, so he was quickly intubated and ventilated and brought to us via the Emergency Department.

He was placed on full life support, the hiss of the ventilator breathing for him, the drugs keeping his heart beating, all for nothing. Mr Barleymow would never awake from his coma, and his family would always know that his death was his choice. He chose to die rather than face them with the fact that the farm was failing and the banks were preparing to forclose.

The Barleymow family made the brave decision to donate his strong healthy organs so that others who wanted to live could do so and then they left the unit, arms around each other, to face an uncertain future, a vacant place always present at their table, the spectre of that final choice never far away. But as I watched them go, clinging to each other in their grief, as a drowning man clings to a life raft, I got the feeling that they would eventually be okay.

The only saving grace about such bitter ends as these is that usually suicide victims are young and otherwise healthy, so that their organs are perfect for donation. This may seem a grisly aspect to consider, but in my experience it may be the only comfort a family can take in the uniquely dark days that always follow a death by choice.

We can close this chapter of grief and shadow with the respite of the fact that, when the content of thousands of suicide notes were studied, the most repeated word contained within them was the word 'love'. And so we must conclude that for the majority of the tortured souls who choose to leave their bodies and their families far too soon, their pitifully twisted intention is to save their loved ones from living with the continuous pain that their own lives have become.

I remove my metaphorical hat in honour of that darkly beautiful last wish and drop to my knees in gratitude that my own life does not carry the all too heavy blight of mental illness.

8

An Organ Shared is a Problem Solved

I can still see her now, a frail little old lady with a tight grey bun and an even tighter, greyer face wearing the checkered woolly coat in old lady beige, vintage cream, weathered brown, and decorated with a strange display of Victorian oranges that looked authentic to the era it had come from. Thick stewed tea coloured tights encased her legs loosely and her feet were shrouded in the old brown lace ups which finished off her uniform of the classic elderly lady. She was fiddling in her cracked leather handbag among the old papers and receipts, softened with age, which would probably live longer in that bag than the purchases they referred to. The scent of parma violets and lavender water exuded from the bag and hung in the air as the Intensive Care Consultant gently broke the news that her husband of fifty five years would not last the night.

I thought she was distracting herself from the devastating news and tried to bring her back into the moment by passing her a tissue, but she didn't seem to notice me as, at last, she found what she was looking for and slid it across the table towards us.

A scruffy and battered Donor Card representing the most beautiful and unselfish gift any human being can bestow upon another.

The very gift of life.

I am always amazed that, at such a time of acute horror and loss, anyone can find a space in their own all encompassing grief and shock to contemplate the suffering of strangers; but they do, and it is a thing that moves me more than any other human act.

'If there's anything you can use...it's what he would have wanted".

The words tumbled out as her trembling fingers left the Donor Card bearing her husband's name and signature on the bare wooden table and silence echoed in that awful room. Tastefully decorated in pastel colours, the floral sofa held it's matching floral cushions tightly in its corners, and the only dead giveaway to the room's dreadful purpose were the boxes of tissues dotted at hand-reach intervals. Every acute area of any hospital will have at least one of these rooms, and I, for one, feel sorry for them. They have tried to be bright and welcoming, cheerful even. But the shock, sadness, hopelessness, desperation and the flood of tears which have been shed here has soaked through the floral cushions and the other tasteful items of furniture to seep into the very walls themselves. There is a reason these rooms are unofficially called 'The Bad News Room' and should you ever be unlucky enough to be shown into one of them, you will know exactly what I mean.

As for the brave occupant of the 'Bad News Room', on this particular night, her ancient wrinkled hand clutching the bent and battered piece of card that was touched by magic and became a priceless treasure, worthless if kept, a gift of unspeakable magnitude if given freely away.

This old couple saved the lives of four people that night, all of whom went home to their families, picked up the threads of their lives, and carried on with the job of living. But I know for sure that those lives will be lived with an extra passion, an extra joy; every day another beautiful gift, every sunrise, every Christmas. A quiet moment of deep gratification and humble thanks to an unknown grey gentleman and an unknown grey lady who bravely went home alone.

The whole concept of donating ones organs to another when you can't use them any more still makes the hairs on the back of my neck stand up.

However life ends, with a whimper or a bang, it's always sad. However long life is, it's never quite long enough.

But for me, the possibility of organ donation changes that somewhat. The silence of a life drawing to its close and the complete absence of any sound, a respectful world retreating for a moment to allow a soul to liberate itself from the faithful body that has served it for so long. Then the imaginining of the distant bleep of pagers, the far away thought of mobiles chiming that special ringtone saved for just this moment, the sound of the suddenly hopeful climbing into cars, taxi's and ambulances clutching battered suitcases and bags that have been sitting by the front door for months or even years. The collective hopeful whisper; "This could be it, Oh God please let this be it".

The whispers of hope.

Often we have to go to great lengths to track down the next of kin of a dying person to ask that oh so difficult question required by British Law at this time, as we have an opt-in system, which states that even in the presence of a Donor Card signed by the person at the centre of it all, we still need to gain the consent of the next of kin before organ donation can proceed.

Sometimes permission is denied by a grieving family who cannot bear the thought of their loved one leaving this world while their vital organs live on in another body, or sometimes they are just uncomfortable with giving their permission to the surgeon for 'the knife'. Whatever the reason, I always understand, but I always think it is sad. My own family are the custodians of my final wishes that anything from my body that can be used is given freely and I would personally haunt them with the full udder of ghostly incivility if my wishes were denied.

Other countries have a simpler system, which states that everyone of adult age is an organ donor unless they have gone to the trouble of stating otherwise, although the permission of the next of kin still must be granted. One of the most successful countries with the best rates of organs donated is Spain, which has a fierce attitude towards gaining permission. While we here in Britain noodle along hoping a relative will show up at some point, the Spanish Organ Donation Teams are involving the police in their most difficult cases, who race after national buses, stop them, board them, and ask. These guys go to extraordinary lengths to ensure that dying wishes are carried out and this is reflected in their figures for successful donations per million of their population, which are currently leading the world.

Sometimes, however, the gift lands right in your lap.

Literally.

Mrs Feather Boa was leaving the ward on the top floor of the hospital after visiting her childhood friend, Miss Parma Violet, who was suffering a lingering chest infection. The lifts were all busy and she tutted as she waited before deciding to descend via the stairs.

As she descended her mind began to wander, thinking of the bus home and how crowded it would be, thinking of her husband's tea and how it would have to be fish fingers again. Thinking of her son's dreadful new wife and that awful red lipstick that made her look like a street walker, and then suddenly she found herself thinking of nothing at all as a bright white light struck her right between the eyes. A bright red flower bloomed in the centre of her brain and she began to tumble.

Sister Blister was just emerging from the Intensive Care Unit as Mrs Feather Boa whammed to the floor in front of her.

For a brief second Sister Blister's round astonished eyes met the sightless gaze of Mrs Feather Boa and for a moment there was silence.

Until Sister Blister swung open the double doors and barked sharply to unleash hell.

Luckily, Mrs Feather Boa had landed right in front of the gateway to Intensive Care.

Unluckily for Mrs Feather Boa, she had suffered a massive catastrophic bleed in her brain, which would leave her place on the crowded bus empty, her husbands fish fingers uncooked and her sons dreadful new wife's trashy red lipstick uncriticised.

After a battery of tests she was sadly pronounced as brain dead the following morning. This meant that the stem of her brain, which has ultimate control over all the basic functions of the body and without which we cannot live, had been totally destroyed by the haemorrhage. The only answer now was to turn off the ventilator that was breathing for her, and let Mrs Feather Boa go in peace and dignity.

And now a young mother bustles after her two young children grabbing lunch boxes and PE kits, tutting fondly after them as they race each other out the front door to school, instead of waiting painfully for a slow death by dialysis.

A teenager eagerly types out his university applications powered by a new Feather Boa heart and lung combo.

And a grandfather opens his once sightless eyes to see that his new granddaughter really does have his nose.

All thanks to Mrs Feather Boa, who loved life so much she gave it.

There are countless stories of this kind, countless acts of supreme generosity, countless cases of life where there once was only death. They could fill a book. A glorious joyful book, filled with stories of loss and sacrifice, hope and love, which ultimately is what life is really all about isn't it. Maybe I will write that book one day, but for now we will return to the inner sanctum of the Intensive Care Trauma Unit, where another battle is only just beginning.

9

All The Young Ladies and All The Young Men

Master Jack Daniels was eighteen years old at the time of his accident.

A handsome, ruddy faced teenager just about to leave England for a gap year before returning to study at one of the most prestigious universities in the country. Destined for great things, a charmed life behind him, none could have predicted the tragedy that was about to snatch all that from his grasp.

One stupid decision, made in a mad second and fuelled by alcohol, left his dreams in tatters and changed the course of his life forever.

Cuddled up on the lap of his girlfriend, in the front seat of his friends car on their way home from a club, left them unprotected and unrestrained when the driver lost control on a bend and the car careered off the road, slamming into a tree and catapulting Jack from the vehicle, leaving his broken body fighting for life at the roadside. His neck snapped in three places, his girlfriend and best friend dead before the age of twenty, and all who were to come into contact with him after that awful minute, asking themselves who really had the luck that night.

Miraculously Jack survived the night, with thanks to the the quick actions of passers by who started the cardio pulmonary resuscitation that salvaged his brain and the lightning speed of the Air Ambulance helicopter whose medical staff initiated life support and whose pilot whisked him through the dark night to the Trauma Centre. Here, the dedicated team of neurosurgeons laboriously pieced what remained of his spine back together and fused it into place so that the nurses of the Intensive Care Unit could dedicate the next months of their working life to fixing and fusing what remained of his life back together. It takes a lifetime to fix what takes a moment to destroy. The combined years of study from the experts who gave young Jack Daniels back his life add up to more than his whole allotted life span in Biblical terms. Maybe the candles that were lit for him in his local church helped, maybe the rabbits foot charm his mother taped to his pillow did some good, maybe the vigil kept by his friends tipped the balance but, however it happened, Jack Daniels became the only survivor of that terrible accident and he paid a terrible price for the privilege. Whether it was worth it, only his future-self can say. However, no rabbits foot or candles, wishes or prayers, drugs or machines, skill or brilliance, luck or time, magic or miracle could ever give him back the life he had before.

Jack suffered what is known as a Superman fracture of his cervical spine, so called because Christopher Reeve, the actor who played Superman in the films of the early 1980s and who typified all that was strong and heroic and manly, fractured his neck at that same vertebrae after falling from a horse and spent the rest of his life in a wheelchair, attached to a ventilator, unable to even breathe for himself. He died of a chest infection aged only fifty-two.

This was the future that young Jack condemned himself to when he climbed into that car. Stupid boy? Yes, undoubtedly. But who amongst us can honestly stand up and cast the first stone of judgment at him for that foolish act.

Well you can all sit down for a start! And I've already taken my seat. It sends a shiver down my own spine when I think back to all the stupid things I did as a younger me and all the dangerous situations into which I blithely placed my younger self, sure in the knowledge that I was invincible and as I knew everything, I must be right. Nothing bad would ever happen to me.

And I was right. It didn't. My own path was lit by a luckier star than Jack's, and this is why I feel lucky and humble in my nursing of this seemingly endless steam of tragic young ladies and tragic young men whose stars have led them down a very different leg of the metaphorical trouser.

It wasn't all doom and gloom however.

There were those patients whose bright personalities outshone their new disabilities and those brave people glittered in that often depressing environment, like a good deed in a weary world.

Mr Trampoline Man was a case in point.

During a particularly daring piece of amateur gymnastics on the family trampoline at a summer garden party, Mr Trampoline Man had only partially executed a rather clumsy back-flip while showing off his fine ability for this activity to his young son, when he fell on his head and promptly passed out.

Unfortunately, his guests mistook his sudden inertia for one of his similar jolly japes and promptly mounted the trampoline and bounced his body exuberantly. He unfortunately became more airborne than they intended and left the trampoline entirely, landing awkwardly and snapping his neck between his shoulder blades.

A devastating injury for such a young man who would now face life from a wheelchair, unable to undertake even the simplest and most private of human tasks without difficulty.

In spite of the radical change from which he expected his life to smoothly run, Mr Trampoline Man exhibited a diamond-hard strength of personality in the way he adapted to his new, limited life.

In the lengthy recovery time spent with us in Intensive Care, after the initial acute phase during which he was kept safe in a chemically induced coma, he was rarely without a smile. Despite many complications with his breathing he would always have the time and wit for a quick fire round of banter.

If he sensed his loss to be imminent in this light-hearted verbal battlefield he would whip out his Nerf gun from under the bedclothes and snatch a last minute victory with a sponge bullet bouncing off a quickly retreating nurses head.

There really is no answer to that.

But he was a joy to look after and, as he was wheeled away to complete his recovery and rehabilitation in an environment more suited to his needs than the Intensive Care department of a major Trauma Centre, he showered us with grateful thanks and the more tangible version of grateful thanks in the form of Quality Street, bags of Haribo and cheesecake in every flavour. We waved him off with a tinge of regret at having seen the last of Mr Trampoline Man.

No, looking after spinal patients wasn't all doom and gloom but as more of these tragic young ladies and tragic young men came and went from my care I began to silently question the kind of life we were saving them for.

I have looked after countless cases of young men and women who have wrapped themselves around their own cars, around trees and lamp-posts, sped themselves into ditches, bridges, rivers and each other ad infinitum in their all encompassing quest for excitement and thrill. As one sad young face blurred into another I began to wonder if we were doing the right thing in fixing their broken bodies around their intact minds, so they could fully experience every miserable moment of the consequences of their actions until the inevitable chest infection released their spirit from the concrete coffin their beautiful bodies had become.

Then Mr Contentment came along and changed my mind for me.

He was in his late sixties when he was admitted to the General Intensive Care Unit where I was working at the time. He was suffering from a chest infection that stubbornly refused to clear with the usual treatments for such a complaint. Due to his past medical history this simple affliction could easily cause a tragic sequence of events to begin a fatal cascade, so he was admitted to us for close observation and intravenous antibiotic treatment. You see Mr Contentment had been a paraplegic since he broke his spine at the level just below his heart in a car accident on his 19th birthday when he took the wheel after a few celebratory drinks. In one more awful moment he went from being being Mr Invincible to Mr Paralysed-From-The-Chest-Down.

Just another silly boy, just another foolish act, just another tragic consequence, another fight for just another life.

But Mr Paralysed-From-The-Chest-Down had adapted well to life in a wheelchair. He had fallen in love and married his nurse. He had fathered three children who were as devoted to him as his wife. He had started a successful computer based business to provide for them all, and while I'm sure there were things he couldn't do, I'm not sure he or his loving family were aware of them at all.

Somewhere along the line his name had changed from Mr-Paralysed-From-The-Chest-Down to Mr Contented, a name derived from the smile he wore and the smile we saw on his face every day. Mrs Contented came clucking in every morning like a plump and matronly hen, chatting away while she helped him perform his morning ablutions, for all the world as if they were in their own cosy home rather than the intense clinical environment of the sickest of the sick.

Their adult children drifted in at intervals throughout each day, sitting on their father's bed, chatting easily about their days, taking not the blindest bit of notice of their fathers stillness in the bed. Blithely ignoring the breathing tube that had been inserted into his neck as a breathing aid, which threaded through his vocal cords and took his voice away as he made his slow way back to health. The intraveneous lines that bristled in his arms may as well not have been there, and the constant bleeping of the monitors slipped well below the radar of importance.

They looked past the tubes, wires, drips, drains, bandages, probes, monitors and machines, and us. Past the bed, past the wheelchair, past the disability and saw directly the man that lay beneath all that. The man whose soul walked upright, surrounded by these people who loved him and he, in turn, walked tall because he loved them too. And his face wore the smile of one who has conquered all and reached his own nirvana and my face in turn wore the smile of one whose question has been answered.

10

Maggots

Yes maggots. Friends of the eternal natural cycle of life, death and rebirth since time immemorial. Our human nature revolts at the sight of those small, busy creatures writhing away inside a rotting corpse. But as they ingest the decay and digest the corpse, could it be that our revulsion signifies our fear of death in all its grisly forms and our refusal to accept that we too, will come to this at all our ends.

Centuries have seen the benefits of harnessing insects to work on a human grindstone and the rewards have been well documented worldwide. There seem to be no drawbacks other than a rather squeamish gross vibe, and certainly many a person has walked a lifetime on two legs where, without our squirmy workaholic friends, they surely would have hobbled the rest of their days with just the one. If they were lucky.

I have personally seen the wondrous work of the humble maggot and its greedy friends. At our very first meeting I was working a day shift on a renal unit where Miss Lavender Handbag was an elderly patient having been admitted with a bedsore on her ankle. This was a chronic wound, of the type often seen in long term bed-bound patients as a secondary insult to more heinous conditions such as diabetes, kidney failure and a host of other enemies of health and vitality that slow the circulation and leave the extremities without the nourishment they need.

On closer inspection the wound was large and deep. The sore nestled comfortably in its devastation of this human ankle. Tendons could be seen, shining yellow strands rested in a bed of slimy green infection and some of the tissue had clearly given up and died as the wound was edged with funeral black. The smell alone was truly atrocious although the lady in question lay lethargically in bed, seemingly unaware of the slow death creeping up her leg.

The simple answer would have been amputation of that diseased lower limb, but that would have brought its own problems of immobility and the possiblity of a fresh wound for infection to invade. Repeated surgical interventions to debride the wound would also further debilitate a body already suffering and deplete.

Medical maggots, or larvae therapy as it may be more medically correct, as well as more palatable to call them, have been gobbling their way through infected wounds in American hospitals since the 1940's but only broke English shores in the 1990's where they have been used in military and civilian hospitals with varying degrees of welcome ever since.

They were duly prescribed for this unfortunate lady and subsequently arrived, sealed in a large Day-Glo yellow container like a rather small vat of nuclear waste. It was highly amusing to see the staff give that box a very wide berth as it sat on a trolley in the clinical treatment room, waiting for its contents to be administered.

I was lucky enough to be present as the tiny thread like medical maggots were poured into the ugly gaping wound. It was a strangely imprecise procedure, just a surgical sheet spread out under the patient's foot to catch any strays, and the creatures were just poured from a tub into that awful hole.

They got to work immediately, writhing hungrily towards the soft yellow flesh, before we covered them with mesh and a bandage to keep them in place for the prescribed three days.

When the patient was sitting up in bed, feeling a little better, I asked "How do you sleep knowing that you have maggots in your foot?"

Certainly not a tactfully worded question but I was too eager for knowledge in those days to have been able to quell the desire to know the answer to the inquiry which was in everyone's mind, but who were too reserved to ask it. Miss Lavender was a lovely lady and very tolerant with this over enthusiastic junior nurse, and she clearly saw my question for what it was. A simple desire to know. I sat on her bed and she told me she didn't mind talking about it, she understood what I meant. It was a fairly revolting idea and when the subject had first been broached to her, she had wanted nothing to do with it at all. However, faced with the very real possibility of losing her foot, her leg and possibly her life as well as all the complications, which would very likely precede that final event, she had bravely faced the prospect and overcome her revulsion by firmly instructing her mind to see them simply as a course of treatment.

It was the only view to take and still stay sane and her bravery was rewarded on the third day of 'treatment' when the bandages were removed, and the great fat maggots were revealed, gorged and replete on their feast of dead, infected flesh.

I had become quite attached to the idea of this dedicated little workforce and was disturbed to find out that after their three days of work without rest, they were not rewarded with a place in the country for retired maggots, or a health farm for the obese where they would be exercised back to their former trimness ready for their next mission. Instead they were flushed from the wound with saline solution, wrapped in a sheet and thrown unceremoniously into the bio-hazardous waste bin. It seemed shameful thanks for their hard work, which could be gloriously seen as they were evicted from their temporary quarters. They left behind a shining red healthy cavity with neat edges and a restored blood flow to a previously quite impossible wound, which could now be allowed to heal.

I saw Miss Lavender again some months later, and although she was still an in-patient, she looked a different woman completely. Without my asking directly, she lifted her nightie to proudly reveal a foot she would not have had without the intervention of our little medical marvels. She now wore a large white indented scar around her ankle as a testement to those little heroes, her very foot a legacy of her own bravery and a lesson to us all on the power of mind over matter.

This wasn't to be the last brush I had with my maggoty colleagues. A while after I qualified, when I was working an extra shift in the Accident and Emergency Department of my local hospital, I came across them again. These were not the workers I had met before though. The beasts I discovered at six o'clock on a bright sunny morning at the near close of an uneventful night shift, were the fat and lazy drone cousins of my hard working tiny friends.

A very obviously neglected old lady was admitted in the early hours of a cold and frosty morning, her tiny huddled figure at the centre of a distinctive nasal forcefield of old urine and unwashed clothes. It was actually quite difficult to see the nut-brown face, as wrinkled as a garlic clove, through all the wrappings that surrounded the sparse form to keep out the dreaded cold. She even smelt in layers. The sharp snap of frost with a disturbing undercurrent of ammonia and mould with a yet more sinister underlying aroma that my nose positively refused to identify.

I was tasked with the job of getting her into a hospital gown for a primary examination. She lay silent as I stripped off layer after layer of musty old clothes and I remember thinking that she didn't really look acutely ill, just emaciated, neglected and chronically lonely. I vaguely wondered when she had last spoken to another human being before the cheerful ambulance driver on this night.

Her legs looked ominously bulky and my fears proved justified as I attacked the first thick layer of ancient knitted wrapping that was stiff with age and stained with much much worse. The unidentifiable stench elbowed the lesser stenches out of the way and took its rightful place at the front of the queue to assault my nostrils. I dug deeper into layer upon layer of ghastly bandage covering a leg that was growing thinner by the minute.

I began to suspect that I was not alone when the first maggot dropped out with about five layers to go. He was probably blinded by the first light he had ever seen as he just lay there on the floor for a few seconds and we eyed each other in surprise before we both realised we had more urgent places to be and he headed straight for the door I dived back in to the job in hand.

Luckily I'm not squeamish so I worked furiously, stripping length after length of homemade bandage, showering the floor with maggots, who joined their comrade in his quest for the freedom.

I was left with this poor lady's femur in my hand. A light bone, with a dry skin covering like one of the Mummys in the British Museum. The only clue that this was indeed a living limb, was the strips of missing skin from old leg ulcers, which the maggots had been using as a walk in larder for goodness knows how long.

Her other leg was in a similar condition and the sun was high in the sky before old Mrs Nut Brown was presented to the Doctor and pronounced as suffering from 'acopia', literally translated as 'the inability to cope'. She was wheeled to the elderly ward to await a bed in a community nursing home.

In all the time I spent with her, she never said a word to me or anyone else, and as I saw her, wheeled away freshly wrapped in clean blankets, I hoped she would find comfort and company in that last segment of her life. I knew very little about her, but I had the feeling she had earned it.

Now I have been heard to state that I am not, by nature, a squeamish person, but even I had to swallow a mouthful of bile when I came across a most unfortunate lady, who had been admitted into the Emergency Department with 'a stomach upset', only to show me her colostomy bag in which a mass of maggots were floating in the light brown faecal liquid after squirming out of her stoma where they had made their home in her small intestine. This was an awful experience for all concerned, but nowhere near my last, or my worst encounter with my squirmy friends. Let me explain.

Mr Unexplained-Seizures had been brought in by ambulance after his wife turned over in bed to find out why it was shaking to see her husband convulsing in the depth of a full epileptic seizure.

The ambulance crew had brought the fit under control by the injection of powerful sedatives and he was wheeled into the resuscitation room for close observation, monitoring and for the treatment of any further seizure activity.

Myself and the nurse in charge of the night duty, busied ourselves hooking him up to machines that monitored his every physical output. We wrote hundreds of numbers on his admission chart over the next hour and filled a tiny host of small tubes with samples of his blood, urine and spinal fluid in an attempt to find out the cause of his sudden brain attack.

It was after the primary interventions had been carried out that we decided to delve a bit deeper with a secondary examination, which generally involves a more in-depth look at the body as a whole. Many stab wounds have been found during this important task of resuscitation room staff, whereupon the medical team have been known to utter a collective 'ahhhhhhh' as the reason for the primary interventions becomes clear.

Anyway, I digress. Back to Mr Unexplained-Seizures. We explored a large and slightly dishevelled dressing that adorned the right side of his face as part of this assessment. As I peeled back the layer of tape and gauze, a large wad of cheap toilet paper came away with it, leaving the most horrific gaping hole where his eye used to be. The top row of his teeth were visible through the gaping hole in the skin where his cheek should have been but there was a sight still worse than that yet to behold.

His eye socket was a mass of writhing maggots, all battling for admission into his brain and it wasn't a major step of logic to connect this awful sight to recent events and conclude that at least a few of these unwelcome gate-crashers had already gained admittance.

Charge Nurse and I connected in a single horrified gaze and our mouths dropped open simultaneously with our joint stomachs heaving and sinking at the sight before us, dread of the suddenly lengthy task ahead and the probable grim outcome for this sweet, stubborn and fiercely independent old man.

Even Charge Nurse with his twenty year's experience of shocking sights struggled to find words for our patient, now re-named Mr Maggots-In-Brain who chose this moment to arouse himself from the combined effects of the sedatives and the usual aftermath of his prolonged seizure. He asked in a feeble voice "Am I alright?"

We lied through our teeth to that old sick man. We told him he had a slight infection in his facial wound and that we would just have to clean it up a bit before we could get him to a ward to be made comfortable and have a nice cup of tea. He nodded his ruined face in complete trust and the sight of him was heart-breaking as he drifted back into sleep.

We were instructed to clear the worst of the infestation as best we could while we waited for the various neurological surgeons and medical teams to gather, but we were limited by the lack of specialist equipment for this particularly grisly task. In the end we took turns in using a thin suction catheter to suck out a single maggot at a time, while the seemingly endless legions of the others continued their waving assault in their determined quest.

It was the worst thing I have ever done to date, and I will never forget it. Soon, the night shift ended and two new nurses took over the resuscitation room and therefore the care of poor Mr Maggots-In-Brain. I never did find out what happened to him, but I did find out how he came to be in such a sorry state and it's a tale every bit as sad as it is true.

Mr Maggots-In-Brain was a retired builder of a strong and independent character. After his diagnosis of ocular cancer he had eventually had to have his right eye and all the surrounding tissue removed.

His surgery was uneventful and he went home to complete his recovery under his team of local community nurses who would monitor and dress his wound until such time as healing was complete.

As so many of this particular hardy war-time generation do, Mr Maggots-In-Brain took this life changing diagnosis and radical treatment in his stride. He saw the District Nurses regularly for a while but then he began to look after his own wound and turned the nurses away. He felt a burden to them as they had so many old folk to look after who needed their care much more than poor Mr Soon-To-Be-Maggots-In-Brain.

When he ran out of dressings, rather than be a nuisance to his doctor, he began stuffing his wound with toilet roll and taping cotton wool over the top. Without sterile gloves, sterile field or the correct expertise to dress such a complex wound it quickly broke down and soon became infected. He didn't wish to bother his wife or anyone else so he just continued with this nightly routine until he succumbed to the state in which his also elderly wife turned over in bed that and found him.

It's a sad tale and sadder still that it's not an uncommon one to a greater or lesser degree.

Medical and nursing services in the community are stretched. Combine this fact with the indomitable pride of this particularly stoic generation with a refusal to see themselves as either old or infirm and Mr Maggots-In-Brain's tragic story can be retold in any community in the land in some form or other. Elderly people are neglected by their families as communities scatter and divide. They neglect themselves due to an inherent sense of pride or fear, coupled with a decrease in mobility, dexterity and declining cognitive fuction which refutes the value of their stubborn independence and so they are lost to the staff paid to man the safety nets which are designed to catch them.

What is the answer? This question has plagued me often in the years separating my present self from this poor man and there seems to be no real solution other than for us all to look out for our old people whether they belong to us or not, sometimes whether they want us to or not. It's a tough call when faced with the desire we all have to remain independent far into our twilight years, but unless we collectively find the courage to interfere combined with the wisdom to intervene only when necessary, then Mr Maggots-In-Brain's desperate story is sadly destined to be retold.

11

Drunkards and Drugs

I could not possibly write a book about nursing in the NHS today without delving into one of the topics that menaces its very existence.

In my humble opinion excessive alcohol abuse is one of the apocalyptical forerunners in the race to push the NHS as we have known it over the edge into oblivion. Persons exhibiting this tendency can be found overstretching resources in all corners of the NHS, from the community services and chronic wards to the acute centres of Emergency Departments and Intensive Care Units throughout this green and pleasant land.

The chronic sufferers of alcohol addiction can usually be found mouldering away on various wards, their bellies huge and tight above stick thin legs below twiggy arms, their skin as luminous as the glow sticks their limbs so resemble, their sunken yellow eyes dark with the pain that their very existence has become. When faced with these tragic shadowy figures, who can fail to find some pity in their hearts, lurking below the swell of righteous indignation for those who have inflicted themselves with their own condition and painful demise. It certainly is easy to raise the finger of complaint about the drain on services not originally meant for the burden it now bears, but who among us can really cast the first stone. Certainly not myself with my secret love of Haribos, a couple of gin fizzes after a long day and the odd cigarette. Any one of these dangerous habits could flip me over the edge into diabetes, a turgid liver and a rampant cancer of the lung. Who am I to judge? And this is an easy path of thought to follow.

What is more difficult, however, is finding sympathy for the more acute alcohol abusers who can be seen, any night of the week, in any of the Emergency Departments in any corner of the kingdom and all the places in between.

They are invariably difficult to deal with; their problems ranging from catatonic inertia, which can require actual medical intervention to maintain their airway, to the mechanical issues of dodging their vomit sprays along with their fists, before trying to find the vomit sprays in their entireties when armed with a bucket of Acticlor and an armful of jay-cloths. This after the perpetrator, of aforesaid vomit sprays have left the building under their own steam or a couple of other burly steams without so much as a "thank you" or a "sorry".

They are, in the main, a most ungrateful bunch, and those who nurse them back into an upright unit capable of self-mobilisation, while themselves remaining upright with their persons unsavaged and their morality unquestioned can think themselves very lucky indeed.

One night I was looking after a gentleman of a typical degenerate appearance, whose odour lingered curiously on the tongue hours after he had physically left the building. He was a whiskery old thing whom I thought rather cute, as he hiccoughed and giggled in a raspy old fashion all the way through my preliminary examination of his scruffy unkempt person. He reminded me of an old, dried, rum-soaked raisin and I swiftly learnt, that however fond one is of old, dried, rum-soaked raisins, enough is most definitely enough.

He requested my ear for a secret and, indulgent as I am towards elderly whiskery folk who remind me of Father Christmas, I leaned in.

The lesson learned that day and never forgotten was, do not, under any circumstances, trust anyone who whispers that he is really the King of The Little People in disguise. Using my moment of frozen disbelief, he grabbed my ponytail in a lightening flash and pulled me in for an amorous encounter.

Lucky for me I was young and quick and I thank my hardworking lucky star that I came away with just a foul smelling trail of slime across my cheek where his mollusc like lips had missed their intended target.

My encounter with the King of Smelly Tramps left merely a brief and washable mark upon me, but there were others that stayed with me for much longer. In fact I carry the whisper of their ghosts with me to this very day.

Like the case of young Miss 1969, named here so because she shared my birthday, to the very same date in the very same year. In fact her life story chillingly mirrored my own.

Like me she had had a stormy youth, had struggled to find her place in life and had started out by having children whilst still a teenager herself.

Like me she had also lost a baby daughter in the same year I lost my own little one.

There was, however, one major difference between us by the time we actually met.

She was luminous and I was not.

The year we had both lost our babies, I had thrown myself into education and she had thrown herself into a bottle of vodka.

Ten years after our decisions separated our life paths, they actually crossed.

She was my patient and I was her nurse.

I had a degree and she had a rotting liver. We were both only thirty four years old.

What prompted us to such different reactions to such tragically similar events? I spent long nights by her bedside as she lay dying wondering the same thing and to this day I still don't know.

I was with her the night she died. A pointless, useless waste of life.

I went home in the early hours of the morning and just cried and cried and cried, questioning everything I'd ever believed in.

I cried for her pitiful life, I cried for her teenaged son who had stood at the end of her bed throughout all those dark hours of all those long nights, twiddling the edge of his t-shirt with his gangly too-long arms. I cried at the thought of his future and I cried for the lack of hers. And at last, I became angry at these people who lie down and die when they should get up and fight. And then I thanked whatever spirit, heavenly being, God, Goddess, Buddha, fairy or rabbits foot that happened to be listening to my rant that day, that I was not one of them.

Miss 1969 could just as easily have been me. But by whatever divine purpose or random accident had made her into her and me into me, her life stopped that day because of the choices that she had made and mine was to continue because of mine. So this was the way I laid Miss 1969 to rest in my mind, and although I think of her sometimes, lying so long in her grave now, I'm so glad that I got up, got grateful and got back to work.

Some of the most distressing deaths I have ever witnessed have been alcohol related, usually involving patients with irrepairable upper or lower gastric ulcers that suddenly burst causing the most profuse projectile blood vomit or an unstoppable flow of blood from their back passage that is so profuse as to flow from the bed to form foul metallic smelling pools on the floor faster than we can bring towels to mop it up. Modern medicine can go so far and no further and once this expertise has been exhausted and still the bleeding continues, there is nothing more to be done and the patient will die of hypoxia and hypovolaemia as their life blood pours from them and all we can do is watch and mop. A terrible end indeed.

We don't see many drug addicts in Intensive Care, unless they are there for a reason other than their addiction in which case they are so tolerant of all forms of drugs that they are notoriously difficult to keep in a medically induced coma. It is almost diagnostic without an accompanying medical history that if a patient requires an extortionate amount of drugs in order to keep them asleep, then they are almost certainly not narcotic naive. There was one poor fellow who sticks in my mind. An ex-addict who had been clean for ten years who had extensive surgery to his bowel and awoke from his operation in the expected extraordinary pain. He stoically refused all analgesia, even a simple paracetamol, for fear of kick starting the addiction he had fought so bravely and for so long to overcome. One could not help but admire such bravery and we made him as comfortable as we could in other ways, plumping his pillows, massaging his feet to distract him from his agony, and reading to him for the same reason.

Mostly, however, drug addicts are seen swinging in and out of the doors of Emergency Departments far more frequently than the doors of the ICU. They are the victims of overdoses that can be quickly reversed with a drug called Naloxone, but you'd better be quick as the patient awakes from his near death experience, as he or she will be mad as hell to have wasted the effects of their ten pound draw and will usually swing punches first and ask questions never.

One must be careful with ones judgements though, however often they prove to be correct. In one case, a middle aged lady came swaying in sideways through the doors of her local A&E, slurring her words and smelling strongly of drink. It would have been easy to write her off as a person who had imbibed rather too much and leave her to sleep it off in a cubicle. It was a lucky day for her that someone was on the ball as she turned out to have suffered a stroke as she was sipping a single glass of wine while cooking her usual Sunday roast for her large family. This was discovered in time for her to be given a powerful anti-clotting drug which completely reversed the effects of her stroke and allowed her to make the full recovery, that may not have been possible if she had been left mouldering in a cubicle for the usual four hours that time wasters are allowed.

There are so many of these that when I was deciding which speciality to concentrate on, Intensive Care became my field rather than Emergency Nursing. They put me off completely. On one particular night in a busy London hospital, there was not one patient in the endless stream that kept us busy without a break all night, who actually needed to be there.

Between the sufferers of watery eyes, heavy heads, bad dreams, never ending coughs and colds, chest pain of six years duration and a verruca, culminating in a violent psychiatric patient who went mad and smashed up the unit and a couple of the nurses before we found out the underlying cause for his acute rage. He couldn't access Facebook on his mobile.

The police arrived to take him away just as dawn broke on that particularly ridiculous night and I resolved to never work in the Accident and Emergency Department ever again.

12

A Conversation With Death

"I'm sorry I came for your baby."

"No you're not!" My voice stamped its foot at this disruption to my afternoon of doing nothing but thinking my own thoughts, lying on my bed in the nurses' home, the sun sinking the way it sinks every night, for those who have the luck and chance to watch.

Silence.

The soft, dry voice dropped into a deeper tone filled with sweet black velvet.

"No... you're right... I'm not."

A cold hand compressed my shoulder.

"She was suffering."

The cold hand froze my skin and chilled my heart as my spirit felt a sadness so old that it surely must have been there from the very dawn of time.

Tears froze where they spilt onto my cheeks at the reminder of that day, so long ago now, when Death was a stranger to me, an enemy who stole my baby girl from me far too soon. I brushed them away in frustration and they shattered as they hit the monkey-puke coloured carpet like a hundred diamonds on a muddy sea.

"I don't understand Death. Tell me! Tell me how you can do the things you do! I know you to be a friend to many an old lonely soul who has simply reached the end of a long, long journey and are ready to go with you: I understand that, I've seen your work, and it is good. But how can you bear to take the young the way you do?"

"Ah yes. I too greet your old people as friends. I particularly love your old ladies whose big white fluffy hair reminds me of a bright blue sky on one of your gloriously sunny days with just one big, happy, cotton wool cloud skidding across it." Death held the silence with the ghost of a smile at the memory.

"Hmm. Yes I love your Elders, they are my friends and I am theirs. I open my arms wide for them and they come willingly into my embrace. Sometimes when I take their frail, bony hands in my stronger, colder ones, I momentarily feel the warmth in their welcome as we walk away from this place together as friends."

"I understand all that Death but what about the senseless killings? The abuse? The car crashes? The gangs? Murder and violence! The pitiful foolish suicides with momentary madness in their minds and the waste of a whole lifetime ahead. How can you face your part in all that?"

"But how could I not be a part of all that? I am Death! That's my job!"

The atmosphere in the gloomy room bristled with an indignant air as Death considered Himself in my small unframed mirror tile with the rust along the edge and the crack that split His image in two. Time stood still or moved unfathomably quickly, it was impossible to tell which in that immeasurable space of past and future infinities that death calls home. It might have been a second or an hour or a week before His shoulders slumped and He continued with a sigh, which froze a column of air. This snapped and joined my glistening tears on the now damp carpet.

"It's true that I have no taste for these events but I do play the most important part. I am the bringer of the end of great suffering. I arrive swiftly in a blast of ice and it is I that freezes time with a mighty, angry roar from the depths of my robes to cry ENOUGH!"

"And it is, indeed, always enough."

"Often I gather these poor broken souls with more tenderness than they have ever known among their own kind. I hold their poor, trembling, formless beings close in to me, into my robes and into my safe protection. Yes their death is mine, but the violence that caused it belongs to you and your human kind."

"It is you who turn your backs to the hungry and needy. You close your doors on your mad and insane. It is you who choose to live in isolation so there is nowhere left for your vulnerable to go for wisdom, solace and protection. The pace of your lives has gobbled your time so your youth run wild to mix bad ideas with bad plans while their elders keep their wisdom to themselves, so there is no-one left to stand up and shout ENOUGH!"

"Until I do."

"And then only I am left to gather your broken pieces and fold them into my robes and even though its folds are freezing, these poor broken souls find more warmth there than their human frames ever found upon your earth."

I walk softly from your world so as not to disturb my precious cargo. I gently walk with them as far as I can until they are ready to walk on alone as all must, into the light, but I do taste some of the sourness of their earthly suffering in my depths and I find no pleasure in these tasks at all."

"Pleasure is a curious word for you to use Death. Have you ever found pleasure in the course of your work?"

Turning on my side and pulling an extra blanket over my shoulders, my closed eyes giving any external viewer an impression of peaceful slumber, rather than one of a person heavily involved in conversation with the Reaper.

"Hmm... a good question Little One. Yes I have. Not too often, as the human lives you may see as pure evil, only meet me at their end, and their history is usually enough to stir even the hardest heart. I would not deny them the cold comfort of my robe, however undesirable they may appear to human eyes... but there was one chap, not too long ago, in my mind's time not yours. Although even in your transient world his name may still resound in the minds of your living, you would know him by the name of Hitler. I called on him in his most tormented hour, his spirit broken, his body racked with poison but still with life enough to startle at my bang upon his door. Of course I didn't need to knock, but sometimes I do like to break the monotony in my endless dealings with ungrateful humans with a little theatre. So sue me."

I felt the cold air compress me as Death himself leant forward with the ghost of a wink from his position on the hard wooden rocking chair he had perched upon to tell his story.

"Well I came upon that broken fellow while his insane mind still capered nimbly and a great rage overtook me for he had put an unseasonable amount of distasteful work my way. I held his miserable jerking form into my face and roared "ENOUGH! OF! YOU!"

I jumped as Death leapt to His feet and banged His scythe on the floor in an unconcious re-enactment of that memorable scene. Furious shards of frozen spittle flew from his angry jaw and His voice dropped to a growl as he continued.

"And I REAPED his soul from his body with a violence I can bear to summon only rarely."

Death paced the floor with his memories shifting the freezing air in that tiny room.

"He found no comfort in my folds and I took none of his poisoned warmth as I flung us both from this world to the place where he would begin his journey to the next. My aim was to spend as little time in his company as possible, but when we came upon the light he would not go. His frightened blubbering essence flittered about me in its terror and to be fair, The Light seemed fairly unwilling to accept him too, doubtless finding his vile essence as distasteful as I did".

"So what happened to him then Death?"

The Grim Reaper rasped a long defeated sigh as He slumped back into the wooden chair, which rocked slightly and the heavy atmosphere receded as He leaned back with the air of one at confession.

"Well I took him home with me. I had no choice. He wasn't wanted and he wouldn't go! He hid in silence in the shadows for many years, until I grew quite used to his prescence there and he ceased to revolt me quite so much as time flowed on. More recently he has taken to tending my garden and I must say he is beginning to grow some quite pleasant things... pansies I think he calls them... Hmmm yes. Quite nice."

Death trailed off into His own thoughts as I woke up and leapt from the bed, flinging open the curtains to fill the rather dingy room with golden sunlight.

I turned to find the single chair unoccupied yet still rocking gently and the air was still as stale and cold as the grave.

I frowned and folded my arms crossly as I contemplated the events of that strange, unearthly night.

"Right. So I'm sitting here on my own having a conversation with Death about Hitler growing pansies in his garden! I have GOT to get out of here NOW!"

And so I did...

13

Leaving London

I had made up my mind to leave London. This was the easy part. But where to go? I didn't want to end up in another mighty metropolitan city like Birmingham or Manchester, which just seemed like London's little brothers, desperate to hang out with the cool set. London looks fondly down on these capering children and shuts the door on them firmly before swaggering out into the mysterious night.

Neither did I wish to wake up every day in a tiny chocolate box village with one pub and one post office that brings the flags out once a month when the cinema comes to the local community centre to show an ancient movie. The population is exactly seventy four and knowledge of all business public and private is precisely 100%. I had enough insight to know that in order to transfer successfully from the bustling East End of London to that micro-environment may be tempting for the novelty factor, but this would wear off once I had bought the obligatory old fashioned bicycle, the gingham lined wicker basket, made my own bread and tried to eat it. I had a romantic idea of keeping chickens and searching out my very own free range eggs every bright and sunny morning, as country mornings were always bright and sunny in my dreams, but where to do it?

I looked in many beautiful places and found many interesting things, like the grave of the real Alice in Wonderland around the back of a tiny church near the New Forest. I stumbled across a burial ground full of giant black crosses said to be the grave sites of medieval nuns who were burned to death as their convent was razed to the ground after they had been locked in for the night by their Mother Superior who also perished in the flames. It is said this strange and haunting place is only visible on this earthly plane once in every hundred years and it is true that I have since looked for it many times but never have I found it again. But I digress.

I looked around tumbledown cottages in quaint villages and ate many a delicious cream tea during my travels. I was stared at in silence by toothless locals in village pubs which used to be welcoming coaching houses in their hundred years of history, but were now the Centres of Appalling Rudeness. Thankfully these experiences were rare and mostly I did read welcome on the mat, but nowhere did I find the place that I felt would be completely right for me.

Until I stumbled into the little town of Glastonbury. The first thing I noticed on my initial investigative reconnoitre with this charming place, was the beautiful High Street, where the shops are bedecked with fairy lights, flower displays and crystals that twinkle in the sunlight, casting their magical prisms where they may.

The second thing I noticed was a buxom middle-aged lady with flowers in her hair, dressed in full witch's regalia, who lifted her purple velvet cloak and layered skirts to scratch her bum outside the bread shop.

A group of Druids in the brightest white you are ever likely to see outside a Daz advert were milling about near the Pyramid Centre, where you could pay to have your chakras cleansed by a prism of light directed straight into your third eye and have your palm read into the bargain.

I was interested, fascinated and completely and utterly charmed.

The next day I made the pilgrimage up the steep steps of Glastonbury Tor. For once I was completely alone, as you can never be in London and, as I sat at the very top, a gentle breeze wafting through the doorway of the remains of the last Abbey which has stood resolutely in that spot since the time of King Arthur. I looked out over green hills and fields, as far as the eye can see, I saw the tops of cathedrals and clusters of tiny towns nestled amongst some of the most beautiful scenery that Merry England has to offer, with flocks of sheep like fluffy clouds completing the perfect picture. And I noticed that the hill adjoining the Tor had had a giant heart carved into the lush green hillside by the Priestesses of the town and, just like that, I fell in love. And that was that.

14

Life In The Country

And so, the deal was done, the move was set. I piled up my little car with everything I owned and pootled up the motorway following the signs for The West.

Truth be told, I was so ready to leave the constant noise of London, the never-ending drone of traffic and the endless crowds that I never really considered what I might miss. The traffic noise also meant access to a good public transport system day or night. The crowds that meant never being able to be alone also meant never having to be alone. There were bars and clubs where closing hours blended effectively with the opening hours of the coffee shops and trendy cafes in perfect synchronicity and one could grab a burger or a bottle of wine within one hour of the desire for that item entering one's forebrain. It never occurred to me that these beautiful things would not exist outside the M25 and maybe this is why I drove west surrounded by all my goods and chattels with the biggest, widest smile my face had worn in a long time.

I had rented a tiny flat just off the main square in Glastonbury and swiftly turned it into my own cosy little hobbit hole by adding fairy lights and candles, scenting the air with incense. Later on, a lucky bargain of a swinging egg chair that I placed by the window, filled with comfy cushions, large and small, wired in a wine glass holder and tiny hidden baskets for secret lollypops and this became my 'meditation area'. Although it proved less a place for quiet contemplation, which I have never been much good at, and more an excellent location for people-watching; an occupation at which I have always excelled, it served me well as a chillout zone, and still does to this day.

From my well appointed flat I could hear the music from The Church of The Singing Plant around the corner, and although this most often provided a background of sweet melodiousness to my day-to-day existence, sometimes the proprietor of aforesaid Church which worships the Singing Plant, mistakenly tuned it in to the radio when he left the building. So the news or the weather report would emit loudly from the speakers hidden within its leaves, which gave the game away entirely and not long afterwards the Church sadly closed its doors and the Plant that had received so much adulation during its lifetime was left alone to wither and die in the window, mourned by all who knew it but apparently by none who had worshipped it.

Although I have never regretted my decision to leave the heart of my birth city, the transition wasn't as easy as I'd thought. That first night in the country, I became suddenly conscious of the strange new sound of complete silence at approximately nine p.m. I tiptoed outside to find the darkest dark my eyes had ever seen, coupled with such an absence of noise or life that, for a moment, I truly wondered if a bomb had gone off while I was in the shower and everyone in the world was dead.

The truth was far less dramatic than that. People just tend to retire early in my new part of the world and just as I got used to that, I also got used to the shops closing at a reasonable hour and staying closed until a reasonable hour the next day. If I wanted burgers or wine I would just have to pre-empt my desires and lay in a stock of them early.

I found a job in a smaller Intensive Care Unit in a smaller hospital in the neighbouring town, and although my brash London manner took quite a bit of getting used to for these altogether softer and more gentle country dwellers, they were endlessly patient with me and after a while both city mouse and country mice began to understand each other. I made firm and lasting friends and I was happy.

They taught me that although Big City people have a street wisdom all their own, Country people have a special wisdom too. While City Nurses are more likely to be spending their free time falling out of clubs and bars, Country people have far more interesting pursuits. They bake, they keep chickens, they grow their own vegetables. They even knit, crochet and craft such beautiful things that give these pastimes a coolness that ignorant city dwellers would look down on and laugh at, little knowing that they are the poorer for not having experienced the best of both these worlds.

I, in turn, brought the concept of fifty pence bets to my new comrades. Although I found that while City Folk will bring a bag of coins into work, winning and losing all with gay abandon, Country People are innately careful with their bets, considering in all seriousness and consientiously calculating the probability of how many somersaults it actually might take a person of five feet three inches in height to cross the entire unit before placing their precious coin thoughtfully upon the table. Incidentally, I bet on fifteen somersaults. It was me performing the forward rolls and yet I STILL lost!

And so life continued in this happy simple way and time passed as time does and we all pass a lot of water along the way. It was here that I entered a period of absolute calm, while the pendulum of life reached the perfect middle of its swing and pauses there while it gathers momentum.

Little did I know then that I was about to enter one of the worst years of my entire life.

15

Burnout

It can happen to anyone. Trust me. Show me the worker from the local toothpaste factory who has not wanted to scream and cry, raging at the pointlessness of it all while screwing on her fifty millionth tiny white cap in a career yawning back years with no hope of escape for the future.

Well it happened to me too.

I was working in a small Intensive Care Unit in the countryside at the time and Burnout crept slowly up and took me quite by surprise as it surreptitiously eroded all that felt good about my life.

I'd had an operation earlier that year and recovery was long and slow, far beyond the quite generous time covered by my sick note.

As my health slowly failed and took my vitality and my reason with it, I somehow thought this would be a great time to buy a house.

I had seen and fallen in love with, a beautiful property in the depths of some of the most stunning surroundings this green countryside of ours has to offer.

Sandwiched between two of the quaintest little towns I couldn't choose between for the crown of pure country charm,

I knew this house wouldn't be on the market long so I grabbed the opportunity with both hands and headed for the chance around the corner.

Rightly or wrongly, I threw all my life chips on Red 29 and gambled everything I had.

Of course this not being my year, it all fell through in spectacular fashion and my shoulders sagged as I watched Lady Luck scrape my life savings into a metaphorical black sack and sling it into life's wheelie bin, ready to celebrate big bin day this coming Monday week.

Yep, in a move calculated to swing the pendulum of fate back my way and force The Universe to bend to my will, I had gambled my cosy little fairy-lit hobbit hole and lost. My house purchase had fallen through and my rented flat had been rented to someone else. I now faced the immediate future homeless and dispossessed.

I took a deep breath, followed by several more deep breaths as I steadied my feeble buff and gathered my weedy forces and did the only thing left to me.

I left my meagre worldly possessions in the care of a friend good enough to find space for it and moved into my car until further notice.

My fortieth birthday found me parked discreetly in the most secluded area of the hospital car park, strategically placed near a lamp-post to take advantage of the orange light for reading and, under the protection of an ancient drooping old tree, which would not only assist in hiding my presence from 1 – the entire world, and 2 – everything in it, but would also provide some sort of shade from the sun while I slept after a nightshift.

Grim times.

Foolishly I thought my destruction fairly complete and that The Gods would turn their gaze to another poor mortal to play with.

While I struggled into work every day I waited for my fortunes to change, taking showers in the theatre changing rooms, washing my smalls in the sink and cutting my own hair in the reflection of my wing mirror. In reality I had only just begun the terminal slide.

I may as well have set my sat nav straight for Hell and swapped my car for a handcart as things were about to get much, much worse.

As the dark winter months approached a sharp event pierced the relentless and increasing struggle my day-to-day life had become.

My husband, the love of my young life and the father of my children, died suddenly and unexpectedly one evening aged only forty seven and he took the last of my resistance to my sweeping circumstances with him.

In every way but physically I fell down. The sudden, brutal swipe of The Reaper's scythe that removed him from the same world as me also glanced me a devastating blow on the return upswing.

I began to cry uncontrollably whenever I was alone. I felt lonely, fragile and breakable, a china doll with feet too tiny for the giant steps that just got bigger every day.

The smallest crack in the predictable routine of my dark days opened up into a giant chasm, which my dolls eyes could see no way across.

Work and personal life bled into each other in a way I had never allowed before and I ruminated on my losses which distracted me from my work. Tucked up in my frozen car-bed during long sleepless nights I could read no more than half a page of my library book before my eyes wandered away, hand in hand with my mind, to stare vaguely through the white and green bird crap splattered windscreen at the night. The hot tears would flow without end as the Legions of the Sad marched unceasingly through my darkened mind.

Every patient I had ever been unable to help, whose tragic stories were lodged in the deep recesses of my brain in a locked box within a locked box marked clearly 'Note To Self: DO NOT TOUCH!' flew open like a grisly Pandora's Box. The pale accusing faces of those I had clearly failed marched through my mind as I lay in my makeshift bed in my home on wheels in the endless sleepless hours between shifts.

I never felt hungry or thirsty and so I rarely ate or drank, the thought of food or fluid somehow disconnected from an abstract concept to the actual physical act of picking up a bottle of water that would be more effort than was possible at that time. When I did summon the energy required for my brain to engage with my muscles in this way it may as well have been dust passing my lips for all I could taste.

Strangely, I never thought of ending it all myself and joining them. Not through any Oscar winning bravery or pious principal; my lethargic mind just couldn't bring itself to bother considering the prospect. It just seemed like an awful lot of effort when I occasionally glanced at the issue.

I had always thought that burnout could never affect such a bouncy, optimistic, simple soul as mine. Surely that was a problem for my deep thinking compatriots who worried about their patients' outside of office hours, took their stories home with them and couldn't let them go. Even going as far as ringing the unit on their days off or making feeble excuses to drop in for news of their progress. And surely if burnout, that dreaded complication of a career in emergency and critical medicine ever darkened my door, it would be to light a wick and cause a sudden devastating explosion; not this slow silent deadly leak. But looking back now, with all the clarity of hindsight, that is indeed what it was. But although nursing the critically injured and ill was proving the death of me, it was to be the saving of me too.

Nursing is a beautiful profession in that, unlike my friends in the production line of that fantasy toothpaste factory, I had choices.

As that awful year drew to a close I knew that something had to change and eventually forced my exhausted mind to come up with alternatives that would take me out of the damaging cycle of caring that had drained my life force to its very dregs.

In January I came to a life changing decision.

I would have to leap from the grindstone that was whittling me to death, albeit with its safety net of a regular salary and distant promise of a pension in the unlikely event that I would live long enough to enjoy it. Away from my tight band of faithful friends yet bewildered colleagues, I would go it alone into the unstable world of agency nursing.

The agency nurse is a thing apart. Free to do as she pleases, work when she wants, yet a transient and friendless figure on any hospital floor. She makes up the numbers but is not part of the team. No Christmas party invitations or team nights out for her, but no responsibilities for the day-to-day running of the unit either.

Financially rewarded for taking huge chances with the celebrated notions of sick and holiday pay, she exchanges security in the future for the chance of freedom now.

It certainly wouldn't appeal to all, but from my position, looking out of a bird stained rear windscreen of the tiny car I called home, my world in tatters at my feet and the devil riding on my back, I reckoned I had nothing to lose.

And so I closed my eyes.

And jumped.

16

A New Chapter

And I became excited about work life again. Don't get me wrong, it takes some guts to swing into a new Intensive Care Unit in a strange new city full of sometimes neutral but sometimes hostile and almost never friendly new faces, at least at first, before your face becomes familiar to their faces too.

Looking after a critically ill patient is actually the easiest part, as bodily system failure is the same wherever you happen to be, and the ways of treating it vary very little. But I have spent many mind blowingly frustrating hours looking for such simple things as the gauze or the linen cupboard.

Suddenly, becoming an Agency Nurse meant for me, one important difference to holding a substantive post. As I could now pick and choose my own hours I chose to work only nights. I've never been a particularly joyous morning person and I've always found the generic 'hospital at night' to be a place of beautiful sunrises, lovely smiley drives home past the miserable faces of those heading in to work. Also, the far less managerial presence combined with plentifully more Haribos, formed the framework upon which I totally based my decision.

During my years as a shambling night-crawler, I actually discovered some very strange behaviour surrounding the consumption and distribution of the obligatory four a.m. Haribo round.

Firstly I learned that almost all night nurses like Haribos. Secondly, I already knew that, between the hours of two and four a.m., the dip in the natural circadean rhythm of the homosapien means that this is when the ailing body is most likely to die. I was interested to discover that it is also when night nurses are subject to a craving for a Haribo fix that is similar to a heroin addicts' need for skag.

Thirdly, on close observation, I noticed that consumers of the aforesaid Haribo can be divided into three clear categories. The first type is the most welcome on any unit at any time. At about two o'clock in the morning, they will produce a family sized bag of Starmix with a flourish, open them and proceed around the unit telling everyone to help themselves. This method of generosity does have its drawbacks, however, as if you happen to be busy with a task that simply cannot be interrupted at the very time this pronouncement is made, and it takes you more that five minutes to dash to the nurses station, you will find a scene which resembles the aftermath of a biblical plague of locusts... and a sad empty bag. You will spend the rest of the night muttering about greedy beasts and hating your fellow man.

The second type of Haribo muncher is an altogether more secretive animal. They will disappear at regular intervals during the magic hours and return, chewing and smelling deliciously of chemical fruits; they will have the dreamy look on their face as those who are enjoying a heavenly nectar. There may even be a suspicious rustling from the depths of their pockets, but they will not meet a single gaze, no matter how hard the stare, as these solitary grazers have resolutely no intention to share.

I belong to the third type, which lies somewhere inbetween the two. At some point after midnight I will go to my rucksack and tear open my bag of treasure in private. I will then proceed to pick out all the jelly rings and cola bottles that I love too dearly to give too freely. At two a.m. I will produce my half-empty bag with a magician's flamboyance, which distracts the eye from the actual object in question. Then I will announce the decree that I have bought Haribos for everyone. In an extra sneaky move, just as the hoardes are descending, I will saunter away with the loud observation that some greedy swine has already had all the best ones and you can't trust anyone these days. Yes as far as Haribos are concerned, I am a thing without shame. Sadly I can no longer scoff a bag a night and still fit into my trousers, so I can happily reveal all Haribo related secrets with no fear of retaliation.

The most exciting thing about being sent all over the country to work in many different Intensive Care Units was the introduction into other specialities that my General and Trauma background had not thus far exposed me to. I use the word 'introduction' in its loosest and baggiest sense, similar to the way a car crash introduces a face to a wall. Your common or garden Agency Nurse is expected to be an instant expert in all fields so I began again to study in my free time and fake a big smile to cover my trembles. Somewhere along the line, I knew with absolute certainty that I knew a lot more than I ever knew before.

I was most scared of Burns as it was the area I'd had least experience in so far. So one dark evening I drove to the Burns Unit with a quaking in my stomach and a repetition in my brain of everything I ever knew about the burns patient, which wasn't much and therefore made for a rather tedious journey.

Actually it was the easiest of areas to blend into. I was already well practised in the arts of virulent infection control and I could pump fluids into the human body as fast as the best of them. The difficulty was the heat! The ambient temperature was kept on a tropical setting in order to keep the patients' who had burned most of their skin away at an even heat. The boiling atmosphere was made worse by the complete covering of protective clothing we had to wear in order to protect these most vulnerable of all critically ill patients from any germs we may carry in. After all, our skin is our first defence against infection.

Shoulder length sterile gloves which met and covered our sterile gowns, leaving not an inch of skin exposed, the paper hat that almost met the paper mask which covered our noses and mouths and left our paper shoe coverings a mere bagatelle in the discomfort stakes. Neither could we leave the unit from the time we started our shift at the ritual scrubbing up, until the end, a broiling twelve hours later. The whole thing makes me feel overtired, overheated and strangely enough gives me a fairly overwhelming revulsion for my beloved bacon sandwiches.

Some of the more technical work is fairly stomach churning too, even for a constitution as hardy as mine. Even though I never took an active role in the scrubbing away of sloughy, necrotic or infected skin from an angry raw burned area of a human being, it was pretty awful to watch. Even the doubtless skill of the burns surgeons speaks of a rough brutality more suited in my mind to the Napoleonic battlefield than the delicacy of the modern surgeons' precise and delicate reputation.

One poor lady who had experienced an acute side effect of the negative aspect of smoking, had lit her cigarette and was about to enjoy that first long puff when the wind caught the flame from her lighter and set her silk scarf on fire. The blaze was brief but devastating and she was rushed in to the burns unit in a blur of blue lights and raced straight to theatre where the extensive burnt skin of her neck and chest was removed. Donated skin from a cadaver was sliced into a lattice with an implement resembling a complex pizza cutter and the surgeon fixed his work with nothing other than a staple gun that fired staples into her blistered, injured chest seemingly at random. That poor unfortunate lady would endure regular trips to theatre as her body rejected the new skin, after which would follow months of some of the most painful treatments which would at best leave her horrifically disfigured.

Far more obvious disfigurement was to be found on the Units specialising in radical head and neck surgery, mostly to cut away cancerous tumours, sometimes to save lives but more often to merely prolong them. These poor unfortunates but lucky survivors would eventually be fitted with silicone and rubber prostheses to replace the parts of their faces that had been surgically removed, but until then they would not only suffer the pain and fear of having such extensive surgical intervention, but the horror and revulsion of their unafflicted fellow men who are either too understandably shocked, or too unforgivably ignorant to hide their reaction to those unlovely faces.

It was in that particular speciality that I met another medieval therapist enjoying a modern revival; the leech. I first encountered these creatures hanging from the swollen tongue of an old man, in the darkened area beneath the row of black stitches that told his story without the need for words. The leeches were doing a fantastic job of drawing fresh blood flow into the re-attached part of the severed tongue that may have otherwise necrosed and died, leaving the old man speechless forever. I have since seen them at work even in the General Intensive Care Units of the West Country and always greet these little marvels as both colleagues and friends.

The most astonishing speciality I have had the privilege of working in is undoubtedly the Cardiac Unit. I am fortunate to live in close proximity to one of the best Heart Centres in the country and so have been able to work regularly among the nurses and doctors for whom cardiac surgery is their life's work and their expertise never fails to astound me.

The fact that a person can have their chest cracked wide open, their lungs deflated and their heart stopped while expert hands steal veins from limbs or other areas of the main trunk that won't miss them too much, and these veins can be sutured in to divert blood supply around a blocked vein or artery in a grisly version of spaghetti junction. The very next day that same person will be sitting up in bed enjoying a nice cup of tea and five days later will be walking out of the door under their own steam to take deep lungfuls of fresh air on long walks they couldn't have contemplated just one week earlier. Miraculous, simply miraculous.

But maybe just as miraculous on a small personal level, was the way the regular hours I was now working, even though they were the most unsocial hours possible, coupled with the fact that my work was now doubly, triply interesting and engaging, made me consider for the first time the possibility of living a full life myself. For the first time since I became a nurse, I could now consider the possibility of living to see the consequenses of not having a pension.

A very strange paradox indeed.

17

The Weirdest Thing

Ahh, and so we arrive at the heart of the matter. The question on almost every lip upon the revelation of what I actually do for a living.

Sure there's some ground level questions, "Nursing huh, I bet you see all sorts..."

"Nursing eh, sounds depressing, all those dead bodies and stuff."

"What do you think about what The Government is doing to the NHS?"

And "Cor I couldn't do your job. I've heard the wages are rubbish."

But it's never long before a twinkle appears in the eye and THAT question appears on the lips.

"What is the weirdest thing you have ever found up someone's bum."

Ah my friend, there are many things to be found in that deep, dark place, and the many reasons for them being found there are every bit as interesting as the objects themselves.

The symptoms of a troublesome foreign body stuck in a nether region are similar in nature, regardless of the object in question.

A flush to the face, an inability to make eye contact, the shuffling gait and the obvious paramount desire to attempt to melt into the wallpaper. The croaky mumble with which one must falteringly describe the reason for the above to the hawk faced receptionist at the hallowed portals of the Accident and Emergency Department without whose permission none may enter, are to name but a few.

These symptoms can, of course, escalate into dangerous territory. The crippling abdominal pain as the lower intestine is punctured and blood and faeces mix in a lethal combination which becomes a medical emergency where secret smiles at the situation of this unfortunate creature are replaced by the serious business of saving a life regardless of the circumstances. But these escalations are, thankfully, rare.

Usually people just shuffle in and lie on their side to tell their story while twiddling the edge of their t-shirt and concentrating heavily on the floor as the good doctor forages about in their colon for the article in question, while making no eye-contact with the assisting nurse whatsoever.

The reasons given for the presence of the foreign body in the rectum usually involves some kind of nakedness combined with some kind of mundane household task or activity, such as unpacking shopping or hoovering the stairs. Whereupon some tragic event causes the sorrowful individual to trip or fall, thereby causing a root vegetable or a vacuum cleaner attachment to shoot straight up their bum with neither introduction nor invitation.

Scandalous!

These mumbled explanations are usually followed by a request not to trouble their spouse with this information or their whereabouts, which is usually met with an enigmatic and non-judgmental smile.

This is a difficult one.

While we do tend to have a little snigger to ourselves and our immediate colleagues, maybe a little story swap as to whose metaphorical fish was the biggest or the best, we have no wish to embarrass anybody. After all, what someone chooses to ram up their bum on a rainy Saturday afternoon is no concern of ours, once we have freed and incinerated the offending object safely. So we usually let the poor trembling husband sort out his own domestic issues and try not to get involved with that side of things, wherever humanly possible.

One such individual does spring to mind though, who met none of these criteria.

For one thing, she was a woman, and an older woman at that. Highly unusual. For another, she displayed no shame at her predicament in the slightest. She simply marched up to the front desk with her stiffly permed, grey hair moving not at all, the very image of respectability in a matching tweed twin set. She fixed Mrs Beady Hawk the duty receptionist with a direct glare and announced that she had five oranges stuck in her vagina and she would like someone to remove them in a timely fashion as she was to be late for her bridge class at eight.

This was done in the fullness of time and Mrs Twin Set strode from the hospital, without her secret oranges, took her place round the card table and probably swept the board, while all our mouths were still set into a perfect O.

Apart from that incident, I must confess that once I had overcome the gleeful snickering stage which accompanied each tale of how a toy car, a milk bottle, a jar of honey or a turnip had made its way into a rectum; I reached the stage where nothing much surprised me anymore.

Astonishment was replaced by a mild sadness that so many people can seemingly only find sexual pleasure from a practice which dices with a surgical procedure, a ruptured small intestine and risks a life long colostomy bag. It seems such a huge risk for so little pleasure even if the result is only a quick trip to A&E to pay respects to a pair of forceps, a local anaesthetic and a gauntlet of hidden smiles.

One would like to think that it is mainly the male of the species who would put such thoughts into actions.

It was certainly a man who went to a petrol garage one night in search of new heights of sexual gratification. And it was certainly that same man who inserted the tyre inflator into his back passage and proceeded to rather foolishly blow himself to pieces. Yes, although this is an unsubstantiated account that may well be an urban myth, the ambulance crew that swept what remained of him into a bag said that in all probability, it almost definitely, probably, might have been, a man.

I will not dwell in this murky arena for too long, as it glorifies no-one. I will, however, answer that often asked question once and for all, right here and right now, and I think I will have time to leisurely write the sequel to this book before a tale comes along to top this one.

Drum roll please...

The most unusual thing I have ever seen pulled out of the sanctity of the human body was a dead crow which was removed from a vagina.

There. I said it.

Whether the crow was alive when it was inserted is a question that went unanswered and I think, on the whole, I'm glad not to know. Some things are better left alone, and this is one of those things. Moving very swiftly on.

Someone else who probably wished he had left well alone came to light only recently. A young man in America who purposefully fed his wife into morbid obesity to such an extreme that she was unable to walk and could only roll around their bed while he rubbed cream into her bedsores, can only have been horrified upon pleasuring himself in her folds, to find the mummified remains of their pet cat, dead and rotting between her legs. I'm sure it solved a mystery but left a scar on all concerned.

Somethings can never be unseen, some stories can never be unheard.

So there you have the answer to the most often asked question ever, and I have a desire to go for a walk in the bracing but wholesome country air to blow these particular cobwebs far away before continuing with the next chapter.

18

Nursing Secrets

The previous chapter actually leads rather well into this one, in which I think it may be time to confess to a few dark secrets of my own.

I have discovered quite a lot about myself since becoming a nurse, some of it quite surprising, even to me, and a very few things I have kept to myself. Until now.

I have long ago confessed that my desire to become a nurse was not entirely altruistic. I did posess a high noble unction to care for others less fortunate than myself, but underneath that high ideal there was a definite nosy parker boinging up and down in desperation to find out exactly what IS going on behind that exciting door marked boldy 'AUTHORISED ENTRY ONLY'.

I'll save you three years of hard labour here just in case your inherent nosiness is as determined as mine. It is a store cupboard. And depending on which one you pitch into, probably not a very tidy one at that. Imagine my disappointment, but that's life.

But I have also realised many other little quirks of character that have flourished along with my nursing career. There is absolutely nothing I will not do for old men with fluffy beards who remind me of Father Christmas. But by the same token, a certain type of old woman tends to irritate me, with their bowel obsessions and constant call for a commode just because someone else has one.

One particular night shift on a nameless geriatric ward saw nothing else but a procession of night nurses parading commodes up and down the ward with only a momentary break at two a.m. for a quick tea round in order to ensure the commode parade could continue till the morning.

I have also discovered an inner rage that is sparked into full ignition when massively morbidly obese people speak about their bodies in the third person, loftily commanding me to 'lift the arm' or 'rub cream under the breast'. The body part being referred to usually weighs more than I do and I do feel a sense of utter resentment in being ordered to lift gigantic arms, legs and boobs in order to care for them and lavish them with the same devotion that would have prevented them from becoming so problematic; if the owner of aforesaid body part had deployed that same level of tenderness twenty-five stones earlier.

I also now know that caring for anorexic patients makes me constantly think about chips and if I spent too much time on the eating disorder ward I should be in grave danger of demanding leg and arm movements from an external force myself.

Loud farts in the silence of the night still make me laugh, and probably always will, as do the words 'knickers' and 'Piccadilly' while the sight of a pair of tatty old slippers or a half empty tin of Parma Violets, whose owner will never need them again, will probably make me cry, while the sight of their dead body probably won't.

My dark secrets may well come as a surprise to you and I have a further surprise to add to the collection.

Your nurse, whoever he or she is, is not the caring automaton the uniform leads you to believe. Underneath those scrubs is a real live person who needs the loo sometimes, or a cup of tea, or just a break from meeting the needs of others for fifteen minutes or so. Most patients' are understanding of this, almost too much sometimes, and they don't ask for painkillers as they don't like to bother the overworked nurses, and I always tell them off for this bad patient behaviour. Relieving pain or full bladders and suffering in general is what we are there for, but at the other end of the scale it is not unheard of for a patient to bang on the staff toilet door to loudly berate the poor nurse quaking inside the cubicle for not turning down their bed or turning their water jug a three quarter turn to the left, or some such nonsense.

Generally, if you hound us down, corner us and shout at us for petty oversights such as these, we may apologise for your situation, the NHS in general, society at large, your life, the Universe and everything else that isn't our fault, but underneath the professional jargon we have to spout because The Management tells us to, we will probably be seething at the injustice of it all and want to break something over your head.

But will you know this? No you will not. Because I have also discovered that, when I put on my uniform, I am your nurse first and myself second.

My chortlings at your daftness will come later, my rants will be heard only in the privacy of my own head, my chips can wait, and if you look like Father Christmas and even if you don't, there's nothing I won't do for you because I am your nurse. And I am enormously proud of that.

19

Embarrassing Moments

I'm not just talking about turning up for work with a few random bald patches and no fringe because using my morning shadow as a template for some quick home hairdressing while running to work is not a good idea. Or arriving with midnight blue ears from roughly dyeing my hair an angry black after an argument with the boyfriend of the time the night before and needing a scrub down from six nurses and a bowl of foul mixture made from every toxic substance that could be found and mixed from the medicine cupboard and the cleaning store. A fiery red blistered neck? Or ears like a tramp from the local tip. A tough choice.

I'm not even talking about sidling in with half an eyebrow or a chemical burn moustache during my regular D.I.Y 'make myself lovely' phases. And that's without mentioning the year I persisted in drawing in my own eyebrows with black felt tip pen and lining my eyes with permanent marker after watching Cleopatra bring Mark Anthony to his knees with her smouldering looks one sultry afternoon, post nights. A brave bid for ancient beauty combined with a hopeful but misguided attempt to guard my paltry finances which, in truth, just ended with one brave soul enquiring whether I had suffered an eyelid fire that morning.

These are all perfectly plausible phases of experimentation that I have visited in the past and will probably return to in the future when the moon is high and the mood is frivolous. They are all cringeworthy happenings but they and their ilk occur so frequently in my daily life that I carry on regardless and barely give notice to their accompanying shame anymore.

No I'm talking about those random and thankfully rare events that stick in the mind as large and painful icebergs in the ocean of the more usual shame.

There was the time when, taking an important and highly technical call from an eminent and therefore scary Consultant Microbiologist, so intent was I to write down all the complicated figures he gave me correctly that I completely forgot to keep my tongue in my mouth for the entire phone call, and so flummoxed was I by the telephonic presence of such greatness, I had no idea how to end the call. Eventually I reverted to type, bidding him a cheery 'Bye then' followed by 'love you'. As if chatting to one of my kids.

Needless to say this awful tale did the rounds of the unit for far longer than it was funny, to me anyway, and I was greeted with lolling tongues and hoots of "Bye then, love you" every time I left any room, until someone else did something equally ridiculous which wasn't too long and I was left alone, at least for a while.

Luckily these awful but everyday occurrences haven't always been so public. Back in my student nurse days, while I was still over eager to please and determined to do everything by the absolute letter of the book, I bent down to empty a full-to-bursting catheter bag, using the correct manual handling position in case anyone senior might be watching. Knees bent to full flexion and back ram rod straight I went down. Unfortunately my stiff new uniform trousers couldn't stand the strain and ripped loudly right along the seam between my legs. Front to back gape.

As a tragic aside my stripy tunic that marked me out as a lowly student was woefully inadequate in the bum covering department so as I made my way crab wise with my back against the wall, my self-conscious face was as pillar box red as the cheap and baggy Primark pants I was frantically trying to hide.

Happily the world wasn't watching this time as I dived into the nearest safe haven of the empty Sister's Office, but I couldn't hope to gain any further ground incognito so I had to find a solution to my problem here.

My eyes darted round the cramped space for rescue. A desk, a swivel chair, a photo of a happy smiling family on a distant beach, none of these were going to help me. In desperation I rummaged through the drawers (sorry Sister Blister) and at last I raised my eyes to the heavens and thanked whatever lucky star looked down on me that day as I grasped salvation in my sweaty paw. A fully loaded stapler.

I slunk home eight hours later with not a soul any the wiser as to my mishap, although it was a hollow triumph as I peeled the ruined trousers from the scratched and bleeding remnants of what used to be my upper thighs, my tender skin torn from the forty wicked staples it had taken to close the giant hole in my trousers and hide my pants from the cruel world.

It's not just me, I'm happy to say. I'm sure we all have moments where we could just curl up and die on the bed of nails of a hundred shames.

With the lubricant of a couple of sherbert shandies drunk carefully via a straw through a skin cementing face pack one balmy girlie evening, which found us again in our usual company of just two, Jane revealed to me, that she had also suffered a near fatal collapse of dignity just that very morning.

She had been part of a turning team, where four or five nurses and nurse assistants headed by an Intensive Care Specialist doctor, who are required to carefully turn a patient suffering an unstable spinal fracture. It is of vital importance to keep the spine in perfect alignment throughout the procedure in order to prevent further spinal cord damage and preserve what function we can for the patients' future life. It's a tense business, calling for absolute silence and complete concentration among the team as a wrong move at the wrong time could cause a more catastrophic secondary injury and may mean the difference between life in a wheelchair or life confined to bed.

The most senior professional will take charge of leading the turn with loud and clear instructions on a countdown of three. The broken body can then be turned safely in one steady easy motion while other injuries are noted, recorded and treated. Sheets can be changed and pressure on the skin relieved before the reverse countdown leads the team to lower the patient safely back into position again.

It was while Jane was tensed with concentration, her designated part of the patient's body safe in her capable hands, her mind focussed, her ears tuned in for the command, it was in that waiting silence, that she let go a mighty trump into the tight atmosphere.

The Eminence at the patient's head led the team in revolted looks while heads turned poignantly away from the newly befouled air and maybe most pointedly of all, not a single word was said. Poor Jane looked frantically around for a random cat or some such other miracle on which to plant the blame, but in this pitiful case, she who cut the cheese must stand alone.

Some of my most embarrassing moments have taken place in cars. There was the time I parked in the grounds of the hospital in which I was working at that time. I would park strategically near to the light of the main doors and grab a quick power nap after a night shift to give me the energy and alertness required for the hour long drive home.

It was particularly cold on this mid-summer morning after an unusually gruelling night shift. After battling for the whole night and almost winning countless times and almost losing countless more, my patient had declared his own intentions and died at seven a.m. I was tired and fed up and the traffic reports were awful so I allowed myself the luxury of folding down the back seats and making up a comfy bed with the goose down sleeping bag and pillow I kept in the boot for just such an occasion. After snacking on one of my emergency hobnobs, I snuggled in to the cosy warmth and instantly felt better as sleep gently rocked me away in the thin early morning light.

I slept for far longer than I had intended and woke in a panic, dreaming that I was trapped in an airtight plastic Ben Ten lunch box. I couldn't breathe! My hands clawed at my own throat as I fought for the air which seemed as difficult to draw into my lungs as pure water. The sun was hot and high by this time, beating down on the metal casing that housed me, and I was stuck to my sleeping bag, my hair plastered to my face, the windows misted with my panicked breath and the air turned to custard.

Desperately I fought to free myself from the sleeping bag that had seemed so cosy three hours before but was now a wet cocoon like prison that held me as fast as if it were made of cling film.

Escape would be tricky, as I was lying full length in the back of a very small car with a low ceiling and only two doors, so I would have to release myself from the bag and crawl over the front seats in my bid for freedom. It seemed as impossible as any feat performed by the Great Houdini, but try I must or die in the attempt.

My breath, ragged and gasping I freed my hot, slippery arms and gripped the front seat headrests in my first attempt to surmount these obstacles. Countless times I tried to heave my perspiring body over the hot leather front seats, only succeeding in making them wetter as I slid back time after time, sobbing with exhaustion, frustration, suffocation and a growing sense of fear, until at last, victorious, I slipped over the seats to lie, spent, my wet body crushed and burning against the roasting steering wheel, my legs still stuck between the two front seats, but freedom was now in my sodden grasp.

I lay there for a moment, gathering my weak forces for the final push. My clammy hands slipped uselessly against the door handle at first, but did I give up? I tell you I did not! Determined to my last breath, I wielded the claw my hand had become through the strange mechanism of my hyperventilation, and banged it against the handle until by some lucky chance it found purchase and the door swung wide. Fresh air rushed in, beautifully cold and plentiful over my sweat soaked skin and into my lungs, and with that first breath I swear I heard a choir of angels sing.

I allowed my exhausted body to slither out of the car and I rested for a moment, with my head on the concrete, my legs still in the car, a lunatic smile upon my tomato red face, and I just revelled in the gratitude of reprieve and the gift of another glorious day.

In retrospect it was a misfortune that my fight for freedom had unwittingly resulted in the loss of my tracksuit bottoms which had been dragged down and were now wrapped tightly round my calves. It was certainly a pity that I had neglected to put on underwear in my rush to hit my sack and it was undoubtedly an error to park in fullest view of the double doors of the hospital's main entrance. Lady Luck had surely been elsewhere that day. The only glitter in the poison was that there seemed to be no-one around and if I could just get myself together, I may yet drive away with this awful scene unwitnessed. This would surely help to comfort me later when this scene would play itself back in my mind on the usual endless loop of shame to the mental soundtrack of phantom children pointing and laughing as only phantom children on my mental soundtrack can.

A sudden sound made me crane my neck backwards and squint my eyes against the glare of the sun to see a rumpled old man, one legged, slouched in a wheelchair, parked outside the hospital doors, the customary fag hanging between his slack lips. His dishevelled appearance plus the fact that he was taking part in an illegal activity without shame, did not stop him from looking down at me with the same expression as a King might wear when forced to look at a gangrenous toe. He took a long, considered puff of his vile cigarette before croaking sagely 'Its hot. Innit'.

Enough said.

I could go on, but over the years I have become immune to the internal twist of shame in the guts. I barely turned a hair when, late for a night shift and faced with a dash up three flights to avoid waiting for the mystery lift which may or may not come depending on its mood. Failing to notice the rather rotund matron a flight or so ahead I berated my sluggish self and out loud with the words "Come on Porky, get your fat arse up those stairs!" Ooops!

Which can only bring me to the awful crescendo of this revealing chapter.

I was working a nightshift in an extremely large hospital which shall remain nameless for reasons about to unfold.

It was a brand new hospital, everything shiny chrome and white, where freedom of night movement was frowned upon for reasons of health, safety and security. In the daylight hours these restrictions were less noticeable, but at night the place became a regular Colditz for a random agency nurse without the Golden Ticket of a swipe access card given to regular staff as their prize for dedication to duty and a panacea for their vow of poverty, both of which come in the small print. Like the Freedom of a City, this card bestowed free access to all areas on the bearer and was strictly not transferrable to those less fortunate and more transient who were deemed untrustworthy of even a temporary card. In short, without this magic key, you were stuck. Able to get in with the help of Security, and able to get out by some wiley tailgating, but otherwise movement outside the Unit assigned to you for the hours for which the NHS owned you, your movements were strictly restricted.

This did not sit well with a free spirit such as mine and I always spent every minute of my working nights in that place, desperately thinking of ways to get out during my breaks.

It did not help that the staff on this particular unit were of a kind that did not look favourably upon the Agency Nurse fraternity, the thinking being that we were the lowly prostitute sisters who sold our services for filthy lucre while they dedicated their time to a far worthier cause. Whilst they would speak to us when they had to, we knew that the worst tasks, the worst breaks, the worst patients, the worst equipment and the honorary broken calculator would add up to us having the worst nights in the worst hospital in a weary world.

The atmosphere was hot and stuffy and, as usual, there was no welcome on the mat so when the clock dictated that, by the law of the land, I must have a break I couldn't wait to get out of that stultifying place. Throwing caution to the wind, I headed out of the Unit in search of a healing diet coke from that friend of all night workers, however lowly; the vending machine.

I strode out confidently enough, pressing all the right buttons so that all the right doors swished open, not allowing for the thought that in less than an hour I would have to find my way back in and those doors that had so freely allowed my exit would be somewhat less welcoming then.

I found a veritable treasure trove of cafes, fast food outlets, a post office and a couple of banks on my journey of discovery through that shiny warren. Of course with it being past midnight, none of them were open, and some of them were still being built, but I felt myself among friends for the first time that night and smiled as I swung through door after door until I found myself out in the lobby still not having achieved my goal, whereupon my smile promptly fell off.

I had no choice but to sigh heavily and sacrifice my desire for an ice cold drink on the altar of punctuality, knowing that no quarter would be given to a miserable agency nurse in that grizzled place, I turned my unwilling feet back the way they had come and instructed them to drag my unwilling body back to work.

It was then that I encountered my first problem. The doors that had so willingly allowed me out would not allow me back in without the use of a magic swipe card. Cold sweat broke out on my forehead as I rattled the doors in a futile fashion, as the grim realisation dawned, that I was trapped in a half-finished hospital lobby with the clock ticking.

I looked widely around for escape. No phones. Anywhere. I slapped my chest, in search of the mobile phone that usually nestled in the pen pocket of my scrubs. Nothing. Damn! I must have left it on the unit.

I circled the small perimeter, praying to The God Of Hopeless Causes to provide a quick miracle but all stayed ominously quiet on the miracle front.

The main entrance was a set of two glass fronted double doors which, when finished, would open in response to the mere weight of a whisper of a human foot, but as I jumped up and down on the sensor mat with increasing frenzy, it became obvious that the mechanism had not yet been activated.

My mouth filled with watery dread as the hopelessness of my situation permeated my frazzled brain. I decided that the way forward would be to attract the attention of a friendly passer-by so they could alert security to come to my aid. This would be awful but hopefully my winning smile would win me at least one friend who may yet secure my release without damaging my ragged reputation by telling tales. Ever hopeful I banged on that inner door, waved my arms, did star jumps, anything to attract the attention of any random stragglers from the pub who might see me and effect a rescue, but apart from a couple of cheery waves, my efforts were in vain.

My brain desperately searched for an escape route, and a final attempt to free myself from this awful state of affairs. The only way back in was to first of all get out. My plan was to force my way outside and then slip back in through A&E like a normal person, chat up the receptionist, who would let me into the inner sanctum and I could get back to The Unit that way.

I put my body and soul into sliding that first set of doors open.

At last, red faced and sweaty, they gave in, opening just enough for a small and desperate escapee to slick through. "Brilliant" thought I. "Just one more set of doors to go and I'll be on the outside."

With vigour renewed, I set myself to the task in hand, applying all the mighty forces at my disposal to sliding open those outer doors. After the kind of five minutes that felt like five years I had to concede defeat. I tried to slide out of the inner doors, back into the lobby, the way I had come, but with my strength depleted, there was no escape there either.

I was now in a worse position than I had been in before. Trapped in a tiny glass box. No way in, no way out and time ever ticking.

I sank to my knees in my glass prison and offered up a desperate prayer to whichever deity might be on night duty with me that night.

"Please God let that not have happened."

It was then that I saw my saviours.

Five burly blokes, fresh from a lock-in at The Hat in Tatters up the road, rounded the corner in fine voice. I banged, waved, screeched silently and star jumped maniacally to get their attention.

The Bloodshot-Eyed-God-of-Night-Shifters was on my side, or so I thought, as the men saw my plight and came rambling over.

"Help me...please help me...I'm trapped" I begged.

That was as far as I got before...

"Oh bless, Little Nursey, all trapped in the window," they leered at each other in drunken, fake falsetto voices.

I took two horrified steps backwards into my glass prison as they began dancing like Jessica Rabbit and cooing into the night like fat hairy sirens until, as their uncalled for encore, five pairs of trousers were dropped and five willies were plastered to the window before five pairs of hips begain to gyrate to the sound of much male hilarity.

'Lord. Please. Kill me now.'

But that merciful release was not to be as I heard a rattle from the doors behind me and a couple of security guards who had seen the whole thing on CCTV, had finally come to release the absolute fool who had got herself stuck in a giant window.

Well I was thoroughly dressed down in that lobby before being marched back to the unit, a sorry spectacle of stooping shoulders and dragging feet, flanked between two huge uniformed men to be handed over into the disbelieving custody of the Nurse In Charge amid a sea of stony stares.

After I had explained what I could of myself and was dismissed back to work, I looked up at the clock with the heaviest of hearts, with not a friend to call my own, and prayed silently to whichever God still wasn't listening, for morning.

Some things take longer to live down than others and I must say, I'm still not quite there with this one. But morning came, as mornings do, and my hope is that, in time, this excruciating episode will join the legion of all the other excruciating episodes I thought I would never live down but have ended up living down quite nicely; thank you kindly for asking. I find I can even laugh about this escapade with some of the people I thought I could never face again.

I have accepted that I will always put myself in ridiculous situations but with the wisdom of long experience of deep shame, I also know that I will always have the ability to get myself out, as well as the front to show my face again the very next night.

And so I thumb my nose at the spectre of the ghost of hideous embarrassment, tuck another story under my arm, to share with wine and friends and facepacks round some distant future table as we swing on to the next chapter together.

20

Another New Beginning

Bored.

Bored bored bored bored bored.

I became slowly aware that my long relationship with Intensive Care Nursing was drifting into a rut. Patients followed patients, their faces blending one into another as cases followed cases and my auto-pilot mode engaged itself as active interest ebbed quietly away.

The miraculous act of supporting life externally to the failing body using separate man designed machines gently became less fascinating as the years went by.

I stopped learning new things on a regular basis and began teaching others which satisfied me for a while. But as all joys fade into domesticity when enjoyed too often and like the pop star who begins to complain about the reality of long months on the road living out of a bag that lies behind the glittering façade of a world tour, I began to crave a new adventure.

Unlike our phantom pop star, I didn't really want to turn to sex and drugs, but I was unsure about what I really did want to turn my hand to.

I felt I may have exhausted all the possibilities that nursing had to offer and maybe it was time to rinse out my career and hang it out to dry, ready for the next customer. After all, I had been a student nurse, an orthopaedic nurse, a community nurse, an emergency nurse, a trauma nurse and an intensive care nurse. I had worked in some of the largest hospitals in the whole country as well as some of the smallest, sweetest and sleepiest hospitals in the actual country.

I didn't really want any more variations of the same experience. It was all chewed meat to me now and I was thinking it might be time to move on.

But where to?

That question was answered one night when a young man was admitted to the Trauma Unit where I was working at the time, after being struck by lightening.

After being stabilised he was to be airlifted to a specialist burns centre for on-going treatment.

The aero-medical team strode into the Intensive Care Unit just after eight p.m., smelling of aviation fuel and fresh air, looking very efficient in their Top Gun flight suits and bomber jackets, huge red backpacks containing all the equipment needed to save lives, with toolbelts slung loosely round their hips. It was all very impressive and as I took it all in, my eyes glittered with a new purpose.

I attached myself firmly to the flight team, making them all cups of coffee, hand-picking all the best chocolate biscuits from a big box left by a grateful patient's family, questioning them in the oiliest most sycophantic fashion while they swiftly packaged up their patient before sweeping smoothly out to the waiting helicopter. They swooped off into the late evening sky leaving us all with our faces pressed to the window, mouths having dropped open from the magnificence of it all.

When the skies were quiet again, I turned on my heel and actually skipped back to work with new plans to change lanes yet again. Within a week I had found and booked my place on the course that would sweep me off my feet and into those exciting skies.

It was very expensive and I had to work my socks off for weeks to be able to afford it, but the sun shone on my brave new world and it was all a joy once again.

Before long I took my place with fifteen other areo-medical students and begain to learn again.

I learned the difference between the stratosphere and the ionosphere and what happens to the already sick and failing body when you transport it forty-one thousand feet straight up. I learned what happens when you pressurise its chamber and subject it to thrust forces and vibrations. Starlings Theory and Boyles Law became my new mantras, and I began again to wake up in the mornings with text imprinted on my face from the ridiculously large manual I had fallen asleep on the night before.

I struggled with the politics of airspace and the ethical considerations, as I always do struggle with such concepts. We took part in a highly realistic and frightening hijack simulation and an underwater escape during which we were submerged in a huge pod in a swimming pool and we had to release our seatbelts, kick out the windows and swim to the surface before we drowned.

It was all very exciting and my active brain was happily reeling with new knowledge.

At the end of the course, I clutched my new certification and smiled my biggest beamiest smile as the Course Director offered me a job with his Air Ambulance Company and within a week I was striding out on the airfield wearing my own flightsuit, bomber jacket and tool belt. Who cared that I actually looked like a lesbian from Prisoner Cell Block H. I strapped on my huge red medical equipment bag and climbed aboard the tiny Piper Chieftain turbo prop aircraft, ready for the ride of my life.

It wasn't all glittering excitement and being rather prone to them, I got myself into a fair few sticky situations, but we were well looked after by the ground crew and all was mostly well.

I did, however, manage the rare feat of falling out of the aircraft after one mission, past the steps, landing on my head and causing myself a severe concussion requiring the need for me to be hunted down and herded from the airfield like an errant loose cow as I wobbled about, clutching my face and demanding to know who had stolen my cuddle pillow. That took some living down I can tell you.

I also found out the hard way, why experienced flight nurses strap absolutely everything down in flight. Our plane hit an unexpected thunder cloud while the pilot and myself had our shoes off and feet up, enjoying a few tempting morsels from the generous picnic basket we were always provided with, and battling a particularly difficult Suduko.

It turns out that the auto-pilot, lovingly nicknamed George, is super brilliant at plane flying but not much cop at shouting a warning. A fact brought home to me as I was hit in the face by a three course meal and a large steel toe capped boot.

I've been stranded in Las Vegas without a cent to my name, I've been propositioned in Prague, almost kidnapped in Egypt, molested in Milan, ignored in Italy, jostled in Jersey and I've met some of the nicest people in the world during my travels around it.

And without exception, the patients' whom I've travelled to retrieve have always been touchingly delighted to see me, which was a rather new and pleasant feeling that I could really relate to. No matter how pleasant or exotic your holiday destination, when the worst happens, there really is no place like home.

21

Epilogue

So what happened next?

Well I did find love again and now live contentedly in a sweet little house shaped like a mushroom in the middle of a 19th century lunatic asylum with my husband, who in some lights, when I stand back a little and half-close my eyes, bears more than a passing resemblance to Father Christmas, which pleases me no end, and so I do it quite often.

I gave up flight nursing when I got married as my husband does quite like to see me now and then but I'm still nursing around the country though less often now as balance and contentment have found me here. Secretly I'm still waiting for the inevitable exposure as a stupid person who has only accidentally found their way on to the Nursing Register. In my heart of hearts, I wouldn't be too surprised if I awoke to a banging on the door and a mob complete with flaming torches and an ostrich feather quill pen to strike me off aforesaid sacred register using my own blood, but having spoken to many nurses about this over the years, it's a common feeling.

If that day ever does dawn, I shall open a book shop, fill it with beautiful, glossy books and squashy leather sofas, decorate it with fairy lights and serve champagne and cocktails while my customers and I settle down to long luxurious reads. As long as they never need me to do anything for them, I'm sure it will be a roaring success.

Jane followed her dream of emigrating to Australia and now lives in a beautiful beach house in the sun. She is brown and happy and although I miss her every day, I have discovered the benefits of best friends who live in exotic places and have enjoyed many free holidays in The Sunshine State drinking wine and cackling over past times. In fact I am in the process of persuading all my friends to emigrate to places I'd like to visit.

The other nurses who trained with us all those long years ago are now scattered far and wide across the globe. One is busy running an inoculation programme in Africa and sends me a Christmas card every year with the greeting 'Jambo'. Another is in Sierra Leonne with the Medicin Sans Frontier and yet more have taken to the seas and the skies. Some have stayed put and climbed the professional ladder, becoming Sisters, Matrons and leaders of their Specialist fields, and yet more have left the nursing profession altogether to become fashion designers, teachers, wives and mothers.

However the common bond which still holds strong, is that we all hold a unique certification that gives us such a wide variety of choices throughout the world. However difficult the job of nursing the sick, vulnerable and dying, I can honestly say I have never regretted it for a single moment.

My children remain the best of my life and they have grown up to fulfil all my hopes for them, mainly that they become people that nobody would mind being trapped in a lift with. A fact bourne out by my eldest son, who actually did become trapped in a lift recently, and I have it on good authority that nobody minded. None of them are prostitutes and none of them are traffic wardens so on that front, as on all others, I am at peace.

I did buy a cute country bike with a wicker basket on the front as a nod to my new country life and it looks ever so lovely sitting outside in the garden with the ivy trailing all over it, where it has been sitting since the day I bought it. Sadly I never did keep chickens because I've realised that they smell really bad. Besides, eggs are cheap enough at the local farm shop without any of the hassle.

I did make many attempts to bake my own bread and as each loaf turned out to be a brick harder and heavier than the last, I gave my final try to Satan to use as a new door knocker for Hell's own gate and put the responsibility for our morning toast firmly on Mr Bun the Baker's shoulders.

As for the obligatory gingham lined basket, I've decided I would look ridiculous lugging a basket, I'm just not the country basket type. Plus I've got a very lovely new Ted Baker tote bag that would totally clash, so I've decided that more of a City-Country fusion style will work out best for me.

All in all things haven't worked out entirely to plan, and some things haven't worked out exactly as I'd hoped, but then I did inherit an unexpected six-toed cat who leaves me lovely presents of bird heads and mouse guts in the most unlikely and frankly unwanted places, along with his ancient, skeletal brother who spends his retirement days teaching the new country kittens to cross the road which entertains me no end, as I am at heart, a simple soul. I learned to brew my own cider and detect the smell of bats in under a second so I can be off before I actually see any bats, so I choose to believe that it all evens itself out in the end.

Just by putting one foot in front of the other, the dark woods have became just trees and gradually these have thinned out into a wide open breathing space in which I can rest and reflect on my journey so far, while the pendulum of life is perfectly balanced for an all too brief time while it gathers momentum for the next upswing and I find myself embarking on a new adventure.

Maybe the sky is not the limit after all. Maybe they need nurses in space…interesting thought.

At least for now I'm satisfied that I can look my talented, beautiful and wonderfully eccentric sisters and my oh so charming brother directly in the eye, because I am no longer The Second One. I have found my place at last.

Portrait of the author reproduced with the kind permission of the artist, Ms K. J. Gilchrist.